Smarter Bets
THE EXACTA WAY

A Simple Process for Picking Horse Race Winners

by Keith Hoffman
The 'Derbyman'

www.TheDerbyFan.com

Copyright © 2016 Keith Hoffman

All rights reserved.

Including the right to reproduce this book or portions thereof, in any form.

ISBN-13: 978-1490965451

Second Edition

Author's Websites:
http://www.thederbyfan.com
http://keiththederbyman.com

COMMONWEALTH OF KENTUCKY

STEVEN L. BESHEAR
GOVERNOR

To All To Whom These Presents Shall Come, Greeting: Know Ye, That

Honorable Keith Hoffman

Is Commissioned A

KENTUCKY COLONEL

I hereby confer this honor with all the rights, privileges and responsibilities thereunto appertaining.

In testimony whereof, I have caused these letters to be made patent, and the seal of the Commonwealth to be hereunto affixed. Done at Frankfort, the 14th day of May in the year of our Lord two thousand and eight and in the 216th year of the Commonwealth.

By the Governor - Steven L. Beshear
Secretary of State - Trey Grayson

Keith Hoffman
Kentucky Colonel

Appointment by Steven L. Beshear
Governor of Kentucky

May 14, 2008

DEDICATIONS

Over the years, it's been a pleasure to share my thoughts with friends and family who were interested in how I go about picking horses and winning races. In response, I've put together this book and am happy to now share my well-honed personal formula for wagering. I hope you enjoy reading it and gain valuable knowledge to help you make Smarter Bets – the Exacta Way.

A few people who should be mentioned including three of my oldest friends: Murs, Gels and, especially, Vito. If it wasn't for you, I never would have gone to the track in the first place. I also thank Doc, who awoke my interest and eventual passion for thoroughbred racing by taking me to the Kentucky Derby for the first time in 1974.

I'd be remiss to not thank my immediate family, especially my wife Laurie, a very special person who holds a tender place in my heart.

Next are my two fantastic children. Philip, fondly known as 'PJ,' was named after my grandfather Philip Hoffman, who was the biggest influence in my life. As was mentioned in the film 'My Big Fat Greek Wedding,' the name Philip originates from the Greek name Philippos (Φιλιππος), which means 'friend of horses.' It's composed of the elements 'philos' (φιλος), or 'friend,' and 'hippos' ('ιππος), or 'horse.' I can think of no better name for my first-born child.

My loving and caring daughter Cristina is so much like me, it's scary. She's the one I affectionately call my 'love child.' Both of my children are extremely important in my life and mean the world to me. Each is a uniquely different individual, yet they are so much alike in other ways.

I also thank my dad, Ken, fondly known as 'Papa K,' who gave his blessing for me to attend my first Kentucky Derby, albeit one year after I first wanted to go.

Long after my parents' divorce, my wonderful mother, Agnes, began to date a great guy by the name of George Anderson. George tracked the results of thousands of horse races, looking at statistics and determining the percentage of wins directly related to a horse's post position. In time, George told me he thought I was the best handicapper in the world. I'm not sure that statement is completely true, but I can tell you George was pretty close in his assessment.

My sister Shauna has always been a part of my horse racing stories. Although she seldom joins me in Louisville on the first Saturday in May at the Kentucky Derby, we used to chat every year on Derby day for exactly 10 minutes. That was because there formerly was a paddock payphone that cost 25 cents for a 10-minute call. Thank you Bell South!

I have two brothers, Kerry and Craig, both of whom are special to me in different ways. Just like PJ and Cristina, they are both uniquely different from each other and mean the world to me. Thank you both for being there with me, from our childhood to this moment.

It was my brother-in-law, Bert Grimm, following years of encouragement, who suggested I write this book. Over the years, Bert and I have discussed some crazy ideas and potential business ventures we could do together. But following all this, I came to the realization that it was time to share my horse racing wisdom in a book.

My close friend Jim Provenzale, who is a great business person and father, has helped me over the years with marketing and other business materials, including an impressive concept for my wine label. When I asked Jim to work on it, he came up with the perfect design. As part of his creative genius, he also designed the cover of this book and my second book, 'Inside the Sport of Kings'. Thank you, Jim, for all you have done!

Finally, I want to mention my closest longtime friend, Bruce Rosenstein, fondly known as 'Rosie.' Over the years, we both have moved across the country but always stayed friends. Rosie and I have enjoyed a lot of good times together over the years and I appreciate his friendship.

CONTENTS

1 Aaaaand – They're Off! 1
2 The Pari-Mutuel System 7
3 The Art of the Exacta 9
4 Exacta Strategy 12
5 Strategy and Evaluation 15
6 At First Glance 19
7 Dissecting the Race 26
8 Class, Pace and How They Race 37
9 Finalizing the Choices 50
10 Wanna Bet? 57
11 The Kentucky Derby – Then and Now . . 62
12 The Payoff 78

CHAPTER 1

AAAAAND – THEY'RE OFF!

My intent in writing this book is two-fold. First, I'd like to help you understand the factors that will help you pick your exacta winners. Horse players recognize ways of making money. Some bettors use calculated wagering systems and others use random, unconventional systems. But if you really want to improve your chances of winning, you will need more data than what the public can see. The smarter bettors always soak up information and learn from others, adapting it to their way of betting. It takes skill to understand and analyze the critical information necessary for making a profitable pick. For many bettors, this is an area where they have room for improvement.

My second goal with this book is to explain the right tools that will help you make your picks. The Daily Racing Form is by far the most useful piece of literature I use to successfully handicap my winners. By using the DRF and other angles, you can analyze data that will not only be helpful, but necessary when you make your wagers. By learning to use quantifiable information in making your picks, it's my hope that you gain some valuable knowledge and also make some money along the way.

As a race horse owner and horse racing enthusiast for over 40 years, these following insights will help you make 'Smarter Bets – the Exacta Way.'

I began my horse racing experiences in high school in the mid-1970s. Growing up in the south suburbs of Chicago, many of my friends liked to gamble. We loved to play cards once a week and really enjoyed going to the racetrack and the thrill of it.

At first, we visited harness race tracks, mainly Maywood, Sportsman's and Washington Park. After developing more interest in the races, we began to go frequent Hawthorne and Arlington Park Racetracks, which were primarily for thoroughbreds and all located in the Chicago area. But the harness tracks were more convenient because they were closer to home, had evening sessions and were open on weekends. For us high school kids, this was much easier and a better fit for our youthful schedules.

I discovered there was a big difference between harness races and thoroughbred races. The horses in harness races usually ran about once a week, as compared to thoroughbred horses that raced about once a month. A harness jockey rides behind the horse in a sulky while a thoroughbred jockey rides in a saddle on the back of the horse. But the biggest difference to me, aside from the purse money, was the speed at which thoroughbreds ran compared to the harness horses. It was simply amazing how fast they performed over the different race distances. I came to like the thoroughbreds much more, as you will read.

I thoroughly enjoyed my very first experience at the track. A few good friends asked me a number times to attend the now-defunct Washington Park harness racing track. Not knowing what it was all about, I thought 'what did I have to lose?' My answer was simple: nothing at all. That was when I decided to hang out with them and check it out.

As high school students with very little extra cash, we needed to be smart. Washington Park admitted patrons free of charge after the 6th race, and that was our plan. We would enter once free admission started, still being able to see some races while at the same time saving our money for betting.

The word among my friends was that we could make some money by talking to a 'certain guy' who supposedly 'knew it all.' One warm night, we piled in the car and headed to Washington Park Race Track. It wasn't too far from our homes. I lived in Flossmoor, and my other friends resided in Homewood and Glenwood, which were neighboring towns and right down the street from the track. After arriving and parking the car in what I recall at the time seemed to be this huge and sprawling parking lot, we stood outside of the steel entry gates waiting for that 6th race to end. We could hear the announcer call the races over the track's sound system, his voice echoing through the track entryway. As soon as we heard the words we were waiting for, "and they're off," we darted through the gates and sprinted through the entryway.

My friends Vito (Mike), Murs (Steve) and Gels (Norm) started looking for the man they'd told me about, who supposedly had that coveted inside information and who would share with us the name and number of the horse that he knew would win. 'Shirkey' was his nickname.

The boys spotted Shirkey across the ever-so-large concourse and ran as fast as they could to him. After asking what horse to bet on, Shirkey's answer was "Number 4." Off to the windows my friends flew, leaving me standing in the middle of the concourse, not knowing what to do. I quickly followed suit, ran to the betting window, put $4 to win on Number 4 and then went out to the apron of the track to watch for our winner. Side by side with my buddies, I watched this thrilling first race of my life. It was so exciting to watch our horse round the last turn and win, running away with the race. What a great way to make money, I thought! I came to find out later that our 'inside expert' was a coach at Reavis High school who loved the track and really 'knew people.' That experience became a topic of discussion for years.

The most memorable harness horse I can think of was the famous 'Rambling Willie,' who won the U.S. Pacing Championship in 1976 while I was a sophomore in college. He was awesome. Trained and driven by Robert 'Bob' Farrington, Rambling Willie was a National Harness Racing Museum Hall-of-Famer and one-time world record holder for a mile in the late 1970s. At that time, it was unheard of for a harness horse to run that fast. Hearing that Rambling Willie was coming to Chicago, I made arrangements with my friends to go to Maywood Park Racetrack, guaranteeing that we would get to see a legendary horse run a race. We wanted not only to see him in person, but also to bet on him. The thought of Rambling Willie coming to Chicago just made me want to go all the more. And, of course, he won his race, running from start to finish, wire-to-wire. What a fantastic and memorable experience that was! I brought $100, which was a ridiculously large amount of money for a high school student to bet. Even though Rambling Willie was the favorite, I ended up betting $80 to win and $20 to place, just in case he lost. I can't remember the exact odds, and I didn't win any huge sum of money, but the gratification of winning at that time was more important than anything else. Knowing what I know now and thinking back to that night, I should have put the entire $100 to win.

Following my initial good fortune, my interest in horse racing now was fully piqued. Horse racing offered a number of attractive things: a new hobby, the thrill of the race and, of course, winning money.

Smarter Bets – The Exacta Way

In 1973, as a high school junior, my friend Greg (known as 'Doc') had asked me to go with him to Churchill Downs in Louisville to see the Kentucky Derby. He had graduated a year ahead of me, was attending the University of Kentucky and working part time on a horse farm. Then came what I thought would be a once-in-a-lifetime opportunity to visit a world-renowned track and attend the 99th running of the Kentucky Derby, the most famous horse race in the world. Yes, that's right, --it was the year Secretariat won the Triple Crown. I was only 17 years old at the time.

Now, most kids at that age could do just about anything back then. Kentucky was 300 miles away, and the thought of a weekend road trip with fellow buddies at my age didn't set well with my dad. His answer was a resounding NO! But it was only one year later that I again asked the question to my father. This time, his answer to me was different, "You are 18 and an adult now so you can do whatever you want." So the first really big thoroughbred race I ever attended was the 100th running of the Kentucky Derby in 1974. I have been making the pilgrimage ever since.

One of my first Kentucky Derbys – 1975.

It seems to me that there are three basic categories of people interested in betting on horses. The first is those who know absolutely nothing about horse racing but who enjoy an afternoon out with friends or family at the track. They typically pick their horses by either listening to others, liking the colors of the jockey's silks, having a lucky number or just basing their choice on the horse's name. All of us have done this once or twice. I am not saying that an unscientific or arbitrary pick is bad, it usually just does not yield a high-percentage winner.

My friend Mike falls into this category. He plays favorite numbers that mean something to him, like his street address. Mike wins on occasion, but I like having a better chance by knowing how to handicap. Many times I have seen him get the Green Sheet, look over the names and the small amount of information it offers racing fans. Mike will then pick a few horses for a wager. This philosophy of picking horses is not what I call 'best practices' and doesn't compare to my handicapping methods. But to each his own! That is why I decided to share my expertise with you.

Secondly, some people might fall into the category of knowing how to bet on horse racing, but really don't know enough about the art of betting exotic bets while maximizing your returns on investments. I have a friend and fellow owner, Chris, who knows what he is doing but prefers his own style of making bets. He has a lot of experience betting and handicapping horses but chooses to wager win bets, pick 3's or pick 4's. That's his comfort range and he does it well. Chris feels that he has a better chance of increasing his profits because he is more comfortable with his own system. And that is what it's all about.

While I analyze exotic bets like exactas, I believe there is nothing at all wrong with making a bet on win, place or show. But many times you can use the odds to your favor and make a lot more money with exotic bets. When I bet an exacta, many times I also will bet a horse across the board, making a win, place and show bet on my top pick.

And thirdly, there are those who like to bet on any type of horse racing, reaching for the big payoff but not really having a clue how to maximize their bets. What I have found is that most people who wager on horse racing have no real idea of how to make the most money with their bets. They may have an idea what wagers to make, but not how to make the most of their investments. I have seen many people who sit down and look over either the racing form or program, and pick a horse when they really have no

Smarter Bets – The Exacta Way

sound foundation why they picked it. They end up placing a few bets and later making excuses why they lost. So many times I have heard comments after the race like "I liked that horse but didn't bet him" or "I took that horse out of my plays trying to make more money with a longer shot." This type of bettor does make money, but he can make a lot more money after learning how to best work the system.

In any thing you do in life, there are steps you can take to maximize your potential to succeed. When I was young, I used to play the game of *Life*, a board game created in 1860 by Hasbro. The game simulates a person's travels through life, from college to retirement, with jobs, marriage and maybe children along the way. Playing the game was just like our real lives, with a number of good choices and others that may not be as good. There were a number of pitfalls and detours that created both windfalls as well as ways to lose it all. But whichever path you went through, the winner was the player who retired with the most amount of money and ended up in the mansion, leaving the others in the poor house. Winning at the Game of Life requires a bit more than luck. Strategy and financial planning can assist you in succeeding so you could live a lavish lifestyle of the rich and famous, while others falter and end up in the poor house. And like our real lives, using the tools you have available to you makes the difference between winning and losing.

It is my hope that you learn a little something that will make your bets pay off. I will help you understand all about exacta bets, how to bet them and provide three different examples how to make these bets. Each chapter will show you what to look for and how to analyze a race to set yourself up for an exacta win. Like a trainer, we need to train, condition and prepare in order to choose the ultimate winner.

CHAPTER 2

THE PARI-MUTUEL SYSTEM

In order to understand betting, you first must understand how the system works. In the United States as well as in many countries across the world, a system called pari-mutuel betting is used. Frequently state-regulated, pari-mutuel gambling pools money between all bettors. In this system, all bets of a particular type are placed together in a pool.

The initial odds are set by a track expert once all the horses have been entered, usually days before the race. Odds will change on race day. As people begin to make wagers on a horse, that horse's percentage of money in the betting pool also changes. When more money is wagered on a horse, the odds change in proportion to the pool. Each type of bet –to win, place, exacta, etc. – has its own pool of money. Taxes and a house percentage are then deducted and payoff odds calculated by sharing the pool among all bets.

Wagers may be simple or complex, but they work in similar ways. Win, place or show bets are easy to figure out and simple to make. For instance, the simplest wager is the win bet. You are choosing a horse to finish first and win the race. The odds are then calculated on the amount of money placed on that horse as a percentage of the pool. Let's take a closer look at a hypothetical situation.

For this example, the combined pool of money wagered equals $20,000. Many pools are much larger than this, but for simplicity we will use $20,000. We'll say the state taxes and percentage taken out by the racetrack equals 18-percent, leaving a pool of $16,400. If you chose the number 1 horse and a total of $1,500 was wagered on that horse, each bettor will win about $10.93 per $1 bet. This yields odds of 11-1. If you bet $5 to win on the number 1 horse, you will collect $55 plus your initial bet back.

Smarter Bets – The Exacta Way

That may seem a little confusing. The easiest way to see how much money has been bet on all the horses is to watch the tote board, which displays the amount of money wagered on each horse as people place their bets. It typically is updated about every minute.

'Place' and 'show' bets are similar to the win bets just described. If you wager on a horse to 'place,' you are betting that the horse will finish first or second. And the 'show' bet picks a horse to finish either first, second or third. These three types of wagers, known as 'straight bets,' are probably the most common because they are easiest to figure out.

But these are not the only bets you can place. There are 'exotic' wagers like daily doubles, pick 3's, pick 4's, pick 5's, and pick 6's, which are among the toughest. Then there are superfectas, which are bets that pick the top four horses in their 'perfect order,' trifectas for the top three horses in order and exactas, which require you to pick the top two horses in the exact order.

CHAPTER 3

THE ART OF THE EXACTA

Exacta wagering, in my opinion, is an art. It is a bet that requires you to pick the first two horses in exact order. These wagers are more attractive to many gamblers because they offer potentially higher payouts to winners. You may think it difficult enough to pick the winning horse, but how in the world can you pick the top two horses in that order? The higher payouts warrant the risk.

The exacta was the first of all the exotic bets to be introduced by most racetracks and is the least complicated, compared to the other exotic bets previously mentioned. The origin of the exacta is unclear, but it may have first been introduced around 1964 at one of the New York racetracks. In North America, these bets are called exactas, perfectas or exactors. The term 'exactor' is usually used in Canada and not the United States. But they all are basically the same --the requirement of picking the top two horses in that order. These wagers also are called exactas in Australia, New Zealand, Britain and Ireland, and they are known as bracket exactas in Japan. But Sweden is the oddest. Called 'Vinnare & Plats' (literally, 'win' and 'place'), this is a similar bet with the exception of the need to place two separate bets, one on a horse to finish first and another horse to be second. But regardless of what country, if you bet an exacta of some sort, you are picking the first and second place, in that order.

There are three ways to bet exacta wagers: the straight bet, the exacta box and the exacta wheel. Each bet is a little different, but the results need to be the same. Pick the first two horses in that order. Let's first look at straight exactas. If you choose this way to bet the exacta, you pick two horses and make the wager. For example, if you like the 3 and the 6 horse, in that order, you would say to the teller, "I want to bet a $2 exacta 3-6." That would mean that the horses must finish in that order for you to win. Any other order of finish will leave you scratching your head and a loser.

Smarter Bets – The Exacta Way

The second most popular way to bet an exacta is called an exacta box. This is where you choose two or more horses to finish first or second, in any order. The least amount to bet an exacta typically is $1, but it still gives you a better chance to win. Let's take a closer look at this bet.

For example, after reviewing the racing form, you like horses 3, 5 and 6. By choosing three horses, an exacta box wager will represent six different combinations. It looks like this: 3-5, 5-3, 3-6, 6-3, 5-6, and 6-5. So it is now six bets instead of one. With this bet, you win if you have two of the three horses, in any order. A $1 exacta box with three horses will cost you $6. Below are some additional exacta box calculations and the costs related to each bet:

$1 box with 3 horses *(6 combinations)* = $6
$1 box with 4 horses *(12 combinations)* = $12
$1 box with 5 horses *(20 combinations)* = $20
$1 box with 6 horses *(30 combinations)* = $30
$1 box with 7 horses *(42 combinations)* = $42
$1 box with 8 horses *(56 combinations)* = $56

Exacta boxes can be played in higher denominations, but remember that the more you bet, the more money you need to place on the table. For instance, you can pick four horses to box together for $2, but the cost goes up to $24. So the payouts need to be higher to take that risk and bet $24 instead of $12. It may be worth it if your horses aren't the favorite, so make sure to watch the exacta payoff matrix before each race at the track or Off Track Betting location.

The 'exacta wheel' is the third method of placing an exacta wager. In this manner of betting, you typically pick one horse you think will win and pair (or 'wheel') it with others you think might come in second. For example, I love the 3 horse and think it will win for sure. Then I choose others to come in second. I like the 1, 4, 5 and 6 to come in second. To make a $1 exacta wheel, say to the teller "I want to bet a $1 exacta wheel, 3 over the 1, 4, 5 and 6," for a total of four bets. It will look like this: 3-1, 3-4, 3-5 and 3-6, and cost $4. You can always bet higher denominations for higher payoffs, but remember that you will need to wager more money.

Here is an example of a few different ways to make exacta wheel bets:

$1 wheel – 1 winner with 2 horses for second = $2 *(2 combinations)*

$1 wheel – 1 winner with 3 horses for second = $3 *(3 combinations)*

$1 wheel – 1 winner with 4 horses for second = $4 *(4 combinations)*

$1 wheel – 1 winner with 5 horses for second = $5 *(5 combinations)*

$1 wheel – 2 winners with 3 horses for second = $6 *(6 combinations)*

$1 wheel – 2 winners with 4 horses for second = $8 *(8 combinations)*

$1 wheel – 2 winners with 5 horses for second = $10 *(10 combinations)*

$1 wheel – 2 winners with 6 horses for second = $12 *(12 combinations)*

You also can make wheel bets the other way, too. Let's say you like three horses you think could win, but like only one horse you think may come in second. You can bet three horses to win and one to place. The cost is the same as above. I am not in favor of this bet because my belief is that there's a better chance of picking the winner than picking a horse that might come in second.

An exacta bet takes a greater risk, but it also has a higher return on your investments. There are many times I will bet on a horse 'across the board' to win, place and show, along with an exacta bet, especially when I really like a special horse to win. The risk is spread over more bets, and there's a greater potential payout when the exacta result comes in. In addition, I like to cover my exacta risk by placing an 'across the board' bet on the horse I think is going to win.

In the next chapter, I will explain some my own personal betting strategies: how I pick horses to include in my bets, when to use exactas and wagering options.

CHAPTER 4

EXACTA STRATEGY

As I mentioned in the first chapter, there typically are three types of bettors. There are the novices who know little or nothing about racing and go to the track for entertainment, and there are knowledgeable bettors who know how to bet but don't know how to maximize their profits by leveraging the available information and strategies.

I like to think I fall into a third category –the person who knows how to bet, and utilizes wagering techniques well. Even so, I always remember and that although we handicap a race to the best of our ability, sometimes the horses will not run well on a given day. They may not like the surface of the track or not like the distance they are racing, or a number of other reasons. But if you use the right tools, you will have a much better chance of winning. Part of my strategy is to look for value and a good return on our wagering investments. We can always look for the top two favorites to come in first and second, but is the payoff worth the risk? Probably not!

I smile in amazement when I'm at the track and overhear people who think they know everything, bragging how a certain horse can't lose or lamenting "I should have won, I had the top two horses but was beaten by a horse I liked, but didn't bet on."

In my experience, many people think they know everything when they go to the track, but in reality they don't. Some of them do all right, but the majority of bettors really don't know what they are doing.

Watching the tote boards that show the exacta matrix payoffs may better help you determine value. I can't tell you how many times I have looked at horses that I think will win but, because the odds on the exactas aren't good, I didn't bet them. The following in *Figure 1* is an example of what I mean.

				SECOND					
		1	2	3	4	5	6	7	8	Odds
F I R S T	1		155	327	195	98	281	202	199	**15-1**
	2	169		342	190	123	385	270	152	**8-1**
	3	349	395		277	134	410	208	290	**24-1**
	4	126	146	201		49	130	4	50	**6-1**
	5	53	69	79	38		50	26	22	**2-1**
	6	342	302	360	153	86		181	177	**10-1**
	7	145	193	169	44	33	126		42	**3-1**
	8	122	106	192	44	28	122	40		**7-2**

Figure 1

Let's say you really like the 4 horse. His odds are 6-1 and he looks to be the fourth favorite in an eight-horse field. Take a look at the sample exacta payoff matrix, above. First, look on the left side for the number 4. Moving to the right, you will see the payout for a $2 exacta bet as the 4 is paired with other horses in the field. The 4 to win with the 1 to come in second pays $126, the 4 with the 5 pays $49 and the 4 with the 8 pays $50.

Now let's look at betting the favorite to win. Let's say the favorite is number 5 and has 2-1 odds. If you place a $2 exacta bet and want to key the 5 with all the other horses, you will have to bet $14. Take a good look at all the payouts on the matrix, moving from left to right on the 5 horse. If the 5 wins the race, the least amount you will be paid will be $22 and the most it will pay is $79. This happens if the 5 wins and 8 comes in second for the $22 and when the 5 wins and the 3 comes in second you collect $79. This isn't a bad bet if the favorite wins, and potentially can be lucrative when he potentially looks like a strong bet.

Another strategy for this same race might be to bet a $2 exacta box 5-All. This places 14 $2 wagers with the 5 horse coming in first or second, paired with the seven other horses in the field. The cost is $28. According to the matrix you would collect from $28-$134. That would be a great strategy for betting this race. The worst you can do if the 5 wins will be to lose $6, and you break even if the 5 comes in second. The most you will win if the 5 wins is $79, and you win $134 if he comes in second. But don't forget, if the 5 doesn't win or come in second, you lose the entire $28. That is why you need to spend the time to handicap the horses.

Smarter Bets – The Exacta Way

When I have decided I am going to the track, I often get my Daily Racing Form the day before. This way I can spend more time examining each race in depth so I don't make a lot of short-sighted mistakes.

Picking two horses with good odds maximizes your bet and is a strategy for success and a big payout. Not every exacta bet will yield a large payout, but it potentially can make you more money than wagering win, place and show. The first Kentucky Derby that allowed exacta betting was in 1985. 'Spend A Buck' was the horse that won, at 4-1 odds. The second place horse, 'Stephan's Odyssey,' went off at 13-1 odds, and the newly-created exacta paid a healthy $118.20 for a simple $2 bet.

Betting exactas in the Kentucky Derby has been very lucrative for many who have ventured to bet on longshots. Over the years, too many to count, I have benefited from betting Derby exactas. Most recently in 2013, 'Orb' ran down the field of 19 to win the Kentucky Derby at 5-1 odds and second-place 'Golden Soul' went off at 34-1, yielding a $2 exacta payoff of $981.60. In 2012, a 15-1 upset by the name of 'I'll Have Another' ran down and closed to beat the 4-1 favorite 'Bodemeister,' paying a healthy $306.60 for a $2 exacta bet. In 2011, 'Animal Kingdom,' a 20-1 longshot, streaked to the wire and beat 8-1 second choice 'Nehro' to payout $329.80 for a $2 exacta. In that race, the second place horse also was second choice of the betting public, which contributed to the large payoff. But the largest payout for a Kentucky Derby exacta was in 2005, and I was there! 'Giacomo,' ridden by Hall of Fame jockey Mike Smith, was a huge longshot at 50-1. The only reason you would have bet on that horse was if you happened to have a relative with that same name. I never had him in my choices. 'Giacomo,' like many Kentucky Derby winners, came from way back to close on another huge longshot, 'Closing Argument,' who went off at 71-1 odds. The crowd was shocked that the exacta payout was a record-setting $9814.80 for the $2 wager. What an unforgettable day that had to be for the lucky winners. Along with everyone else, I was blown away when the payouts were flashed on the board. To say the win by 'Giacomo' was a surprise is an enormous understatement, but the 71-1 longshot 'Closing Argument' coming in second had the crowd on their feet. I was beside myself. That was a payout no one would have expected, especially me.

CHAPTER 5

STRATEGY AND EVALUATION

Now that exacta bets and some of the strategies have been explained, the next step is to figure out which horses to pick. This may seem difficult, but I assure that you'll pick more winners if you spend some time analyzing the race.

Another betting strategy of mine is to find the horse you think will win, and then find the horse that can beat it. A close family friend, George, always told me that I was one of the best handicappers he ever knew. I could not only pick winners, but I could find winners that paid off with higher odds. And he was right. When I won, many times my payoffs were larger than for most other winning bettors. And that was because I always looked for the horse that could win, and then found a horse that I thought could beat it.

I look at many factors when betting on horses. Sometimes it may be difficult to do that when you're at the track and don't have a lot of time. There are a number of things that will help eliminate those horses that shouldn't win and find those that should. Many people have their own opinions and angles on how to win, but most are not thought through in great depth and fall short. These handicappers fall into one of three categories.

The first is the novice handicapper who picks horses by name, colors or its number. I once knew a guy, Dennis, who always bet like this. His picks relate to something personal like his sister's name, his birthday or some other unorthodox reason. This is by far the least productive way to pick a horse and many times is annoying to other bettors. Now, I will be the first to say that I have done this on occasion and it proved ineffective and unprofitable, with a few exceptions. I recently attended a holiday party hosted by my good friends Jack and Jackie. Earlier, I had looked at the races for that day and actually saw a horse by the name 'Jackie's Jack.' Low and behold, the horse with morning odds of 12-1 went off at 14-1, came in second and paid a whopping $9 to place and $5.40 to show. If I was a big spender and had bet $100 across the board (win, place and show), I could have collected $720 for a $300 bet and made a profit of $420. What a strange coincidence that was.

The second type of handicapper is the one who looks over the choices and picks one that has won the most races or possible purse money. Many people think that if a horse won his last race, he should be able to win this one. But it doesn't always happen that way. A lot of times, a horse has what we call a 'perfect trip,' with the race set up for a win, based on his running style and other horses entered in the race. Also falling into this category would be a front-running horse with no other 'speed horses' in the race, or a horse that likes to come from behind in a race that has a few fast runners that can be expected to burn each other out. And then there are race positions that just favor the horse. One that has a style of coming from behind, or a 'closer,' will be less successful starting from gate positions 1 or 2. A closer needs an outside gate as a way to run down the other horses with little traffic or obstructions.

And the third is the true handicapper who spends the time to review each race and who chooses winners based on facts. There are angles that trainers use to enhance their opportunities to win. Likewise, a smart bettor will pick up things and keep them in the back of his mind when making his wagers. Understanding and analyzing information is the key to maximizing profits.

There are a few different types of materials you can use to handicap each race, and some work better than others. One of these is called the Green Sheet. Condensed and not very analytical, the Green Sheet is my least favorite. Like a few others, it provides few statistics and is inexpensive but nevertheless is a quick reference to each race.

The track's racing program is typical for many handicappers who want to see the details of each race. These are usually either free with admission to the track or less expensive than the next option. It has a lot of important information needed to choose your selections but is missing a few key elements. You can get this right at the racetrack or OTB.

And then there is my favorite, the Daily Racing Form. This publication goes into far greater depth with what I think are the most important links to successful handicapping. Many of the things you get in the DRF can be found in the racing program, but not the most important links to success. Some of these elements include trainer and jockey history, track and surface statistics and in-depth expert comments on a horse. The DRF can be purchased either in paper form or on-line at www.drf.com. Whether you choose to use the Green Sheet, the track racing program or the DRF, spend some time looking over each race in depth. And don't think you can win every race, because you can't!

Here are a few of my beliefs on horse racing:

- It is much tougher for younger horses to beat older, more mature horses.
- You can't win every race, so pass on those you are not sure you should bet.
- Horses like certain tracks and conditions, so keep an eye out for these stats.
- Most good trainers are 'in the money' (finishing first, second or third) about 50-60 percent of the time, and I always watch for them.
- Bet the better-quality races likes Stakes, Allowances or higher-priced Claimers.
- Just because a horse is a favorite doesn't necessarily mean he has to win.
- Workouts are a key to success. Identify whether a horse is in good shape.
- And, most importantly (which was stated previously): find the horse you think will win and then find the one who can beat him.

I analyze each race and look at 12 things before narrowing down the selections to the top possibilities and picking which one will win the race. An in-depth look at this 'dirty dozen' will shed more light on the horses I'll be including in my picks:

1. The type of race
2. Surface and condition of the track
3. Length of the race
4. Trainer stats
5. Jockey stats
6. The style of horses racing (speed, stalker, closer)

7. A horse's money winnings

8. Statistics about a horse's workouts

9. Ages of the horses racing

10. Tomlinson performance rating

11. Distance performance figures

12. Beyer Speed Figure

Each of these pieces of information will provide you a better perspective to pick your winners. Some will carry more weight than others. But when you put them together, they will help you to choose the right horse.

It takes preparation to find your winners using the Daily RacingForm.

It pays off in the end!!

CHAPTER 6

AT FIRST GLANCE

Let's take a closer look at the form. Each race has a great deal of information you need to understand.

There are different classifications of races, including Maiden (horses that have never won), Claiming (horses may be 'claimed' for purchase), Conditional or Allowance (horses must meet certain specific criteria) and Stakes (highest level of competition). Each of these has different levels or 'Grades' within the classification. Let's now look at the specific conditions or criteria for a race in *Figure 2*.

Figure 2

Race 5 is at a distance of 7 furlongs and Grade 1 status. It is designated for fillies (female horses not yet 5 years old) and mares (female horses that have reached age 5). The weight limitations that are designated for this race are stated. In this case, the weight that each horse will carry cannot be less than 122 pounds for 3-year-olds, and older horses must carry at least 124 pounds. This is because older horses are more mature, stronger and more developed than the younger horses. 3-year-olds from the Southern hemisphere receive an added benefit and advantage of being allowed to carry the lower weight of 120 pounds. The example shows that the purse is $1,000,000 and that each horse is paid by order of finish. This is one of the larger purse races and happens to be during Breeder's Cup weekend, when the best horses worldwide compete for top purse money in many different categories.

It is important to note that there are numerous wagers allowed in this race, as shown in the form, including our exacta bets. And for those who want to be sure to not miss wagering for a given race, be aware of the race time and make sure your bets are placed well before the post time. As you move into the later races of the day, people tend to place more wagers and the betting windows can get busy. The one thing we don't want to do is to get shut out of making our bet. And finally, in this section of the racing form, it shows that this race is being run on dirt. Unless it is stated 'turf' or the track is a 'synthetic or all-weather track,' it will be run on a dirt surface.

The next section is one of the most critical to study. It involves key stats that will be the most helpful to you.

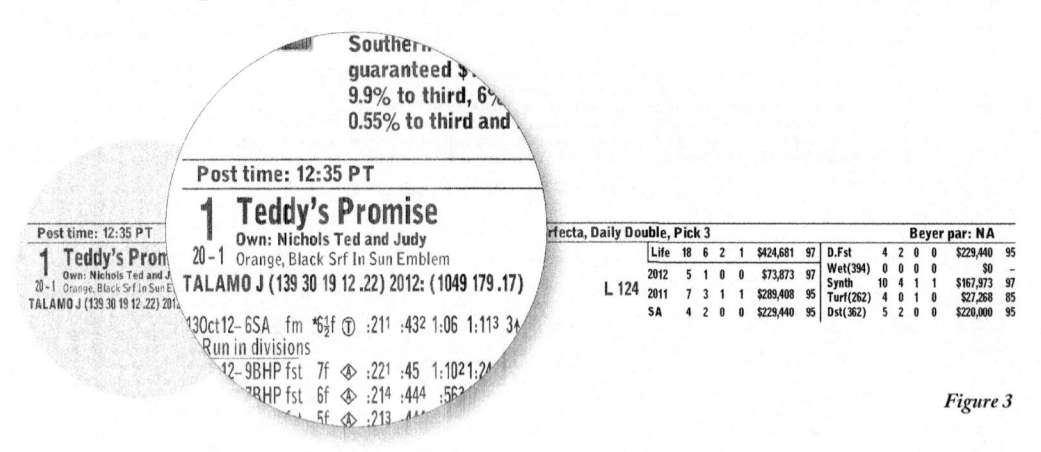

Figure 3

The first thing you notice is the number and the name of the horse, the owners, the beginning morning line odds (20-1) and the colors the jockey will be wearing *(Figure 3)*. Many times it will be easier to spot your horse by the jockey's colors rather than trying to look for the number on the horse. Below this information are the jockey's name and racing stats, separated into two sections. The first bits of information are the statistics for that jockey at the track for that meet (or track racing schedule), and the second figures are the stats for that jockey for the entire year at all tracks. For jockey Joe Talamo, the information in the parentheses reads like this: For this meet at Santa Anita, he has raced 139 times with 30 wins, 19 seconds and 12 thirds. The .22 is the percentage of winners he rode in this meet, which means 22-percent of his rides culminated in wins. The second parentheses show that he has ridden this year 1,049 times with 179 winners, and that 17-percent of his rides were wins.

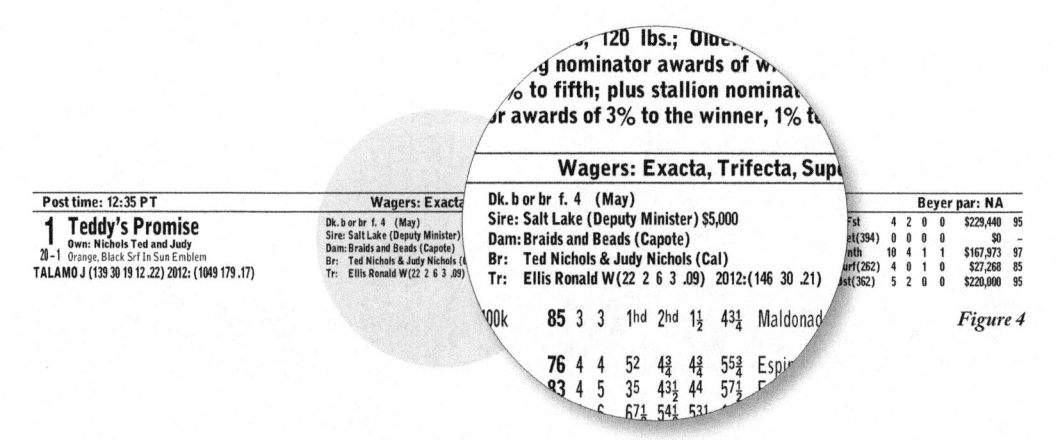

Figure 4

The next sections *(Figure 4)* of the form contain information about the horses and the trainer. This includes the age of the horse, the color of its coat, breeding, trainer statistics and finally the dollar amount the horse has won. Looking at the chart above, it shows the horse is a Dark Bay or Brown filly, 4 years old, foaled in May. Her sire (father) was named 'Salt Lake' (who's sire was 'Deputy Minister') and her dam (mother) was 'Braids and Beads' (sired by 'Capote'). She was bred by Ted and Judy Nichols in California and her trainer is Ronald Ellis, who has statistics of 9-percent wins out of 22 races for the meet and 21-percent winners from 146 races this year. This tells me that the trainer hasn't raced very many times at Santa Anita this meet and only has a small percentage of winners. Now that doesn't mean he is a bad trainer, as he has won 21-percent of his starters this year. It probably means he has been racing in other parts of the country and still may be a decent trainer. Trainer stats are one of my more important keys to choosing a horse. I always favor a trainer with better stats over one who has fewer wins. The yearly statistics are a truer representation and offer a better picture of a trainer's ability to have a horse place in the money. And that statistic can only be seen in the Daily Racing Form rather than a program sold or given to you by the track. This is one good reason to buy the DRF.

Smarter Bets – The Exacta Way

Next, we see the figure 'L124' *(Figure 5)*. The 'L' indicates that the horse uses the anti-bleeding drug Lasix, and that the jockey will be carrying 124 total pounds. This is important, as many races allow different weights and a couple pounds ultimately may make the difference between first and second place. When I look at weights, I always compare them to the last few races to see how much a horse carried. In addition, when you compare weights, expert handicappers generally agree that every pound is equivalent to about 1/5 of a second in time. So in theory, a horse that carries 5-pounds less is about 1-second faster. As we look closer at individual race history, I will address this more in depth.

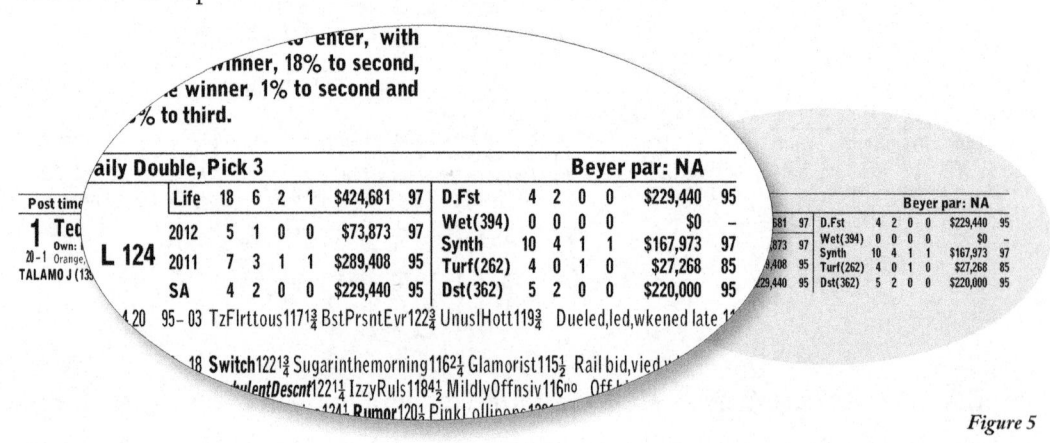

Figure 5

The next key to identifying a successful winner is to look at the horse's actual statistics. We can see the number of races and how much money a horse has won. This not only shows me performance, but how much money was won per race on a given track surface.

'Teddy's Promise' has raced 18 times over her lifetime. She has won six of them, or 33-percent. She has two seconds and one third-place finish, has made $424,681 and her best Beyer's figure is 97. This tells me that she has been first, second or third 50-percent of the time. I simply add up the in-the-money finishes and divide by the total. In this case it is 9 out of 18 races. Next, I look at each year and the stats for the current year. In 2012, she raced five times with only one win and a total income of $73,873. Now, those winnings are not too shabby, but her total number of races in the money seems to be low in comparison to what I like to see from a horse. Below those stats, I see that 'Teddy's Promise' raced seven times in 2011, with three wins, one second and one third, for a total of $289,408 and a Beyer's rating of 95. That equates to being in the money 71-percent of the time and an average of $41,344 per race. To calculate this, I divided the total money winnings into the amount of races. $289,408 divided by seven equals $41,344. But one of the most important things I look at is the number of races at a particular track. At Santa Anita (SA, bottom of the list), he raced four times with two wins and earnings of $229,440. This tells me that she likes to race at Santa Anita. That is important when comparing horses. Remember that horses race their best when they are familiar with and like the track surface. Many times I have bet on a horse that might not look as strong as the others but loves to finish in the money at a particular track.

Now take a good look at the next set of stats *(Figure 6)*, which tell the type of track and weather conditions. This is a critical factor because some horses just like certain surfaces.

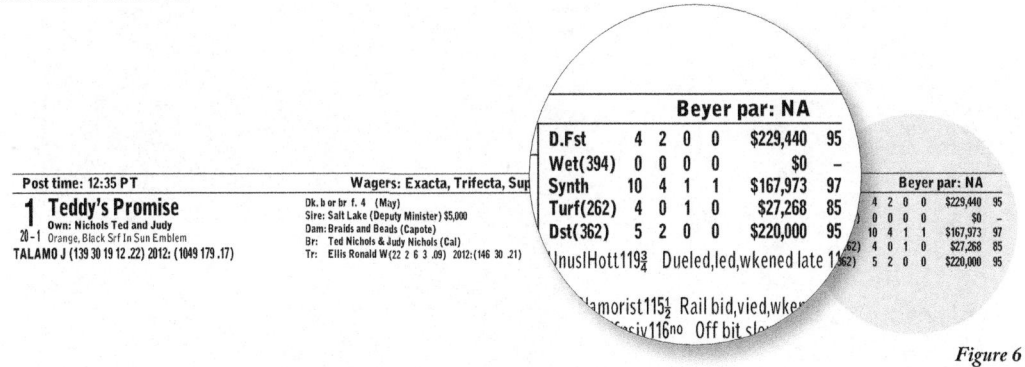

Figure 6

Here we see in the top right portion of the form that on a fast dirt track (D.Fst), 'Teddy's Promise' has raced four times with two wins and no seconds or thirds. She won $229,440 on dirt, which is equivalent to $57,350 per race and $114,720 per win –pretty decent for a 4-year-old filly.

The parentheses following a particular track surface contain a number (the 'Tomlinson Rating') that shows how a horse should perform, based on his bloodline. In this case, 'Teddy's Promise' has never raced on a wet track but horses in her bloodline have done well. The higher the number, the more potential that horse may perform well under those conditions.

This horse has raced 10 times on a synthetic track surface. She has won four times, has one second and one third-place finish and winnings of $167,973. Our calculations show that 40-percent of her synthetic races have culminated in wins. That's a good statistic. On turf, she has raced four times with little success, showing only one second-place finish and $27,268 in winnings.

Smarter Bets – The Exacta Way

One of the most important stats to look at is the last one, which is distance on that race surface. In the case of 'Teddy's Promise,' she has raced five times at this distance on dirt with two wins and no seconds or thirds. But she has won $220,000 and has a Beyer's rating of 95. We can summarize that for this distance, the horse has pretty good in the money winnings, along with a 40-percent win record, significant factors when comparing the horses. I always like to bet a horse that has a good record at the distance compared to one that may be in a distance the horse doesn't prefer. Again, I will always look at the Beyer's rating. The higher the number, the more likely that horse has to win at that distance and track surface.

A beautiful day at Santa Anita for Breeder's Cup.

Keith Hoffman *'The Derbyman'*

Hall-of-Famer Laffit Pincay, Jr. joins my sister, Shauna, and I for a quick photo at Breeder's Cup.

One of our personal jockeys, Mitchell Murrill poses with me on the paddock at Arlington International Racecourse.

A nice afternoon with my wife Laurie, brother Kerry and sister-in-law, Greta.

Having a chat with Joe Kristofek at Churchill Downs in the paddock at the Kentucky Derby in 2015.

CHAPTER 7

DISSECTING THE RACE

Now that you understand more about looking at the statistics, it's time to evaluate the actual race and narrow it down to the top horses you want to bet. In my opinion, evaluation is the most important and most difficult aspect where you must spend the most time. With that in mind, let's take a closer look at a particular race.

Figure 7

There are 10 things I consider in evaluating this portion of the form. I now will look for what I think should make a horse a cut above the others in a race. I always remember my top three parameters that are important to picking my best horses. They are class, pace and how they race or 'the ultimate trip.' Here are my 10 race considerations *(Figure 7)*:

1. The class of races in which the horse has competed

2. The style in which a horse races (i.e., a front-runner, a stalker or a closer)

3. Time fractions of the races

4. The horse's Beyer Speed Figures

5. The jockey in each race and the weight carried

6. The numbers after the odds (99-10), which is the Standard Speed Rating

7. Comments after each race finish

8. Works (workout times)

9. Trainer stats and information

10. My overall perception of the horse in general

These overall race considerations should not be confused with my 'dirty dozen,' explained in Chapter 5, which are evaluations for individual horses.

Race Class

One of the first things I look at in this section is the quality of the horses running. Consider that to be the 'class' of the horse. What I mean by this is what types of races the horse has been racing. This will help me to decide whether the horse deserves to be in the race. In the case of 'Dust and Diamonds,' you can look over the races this horse has recently raced. This year, the horse has raced four times. She began this year in Optional Claiming company of non-winners of two races for a purse of $62,000, then moved down to the same type of race at a lower purse of $35,000 before moving up in class. Her next race was a Stakes race for $50,000, followed by a higher-level Grade 2 Stakes race. We can see that, as she was winning, she moved up in class and continued to win. This is a sure indication of a good horse. I love to see this type of racing history as a strong indication a horse is in the right race. Later, we will look at the example of an entire race and you will see what I mean. As you look over horses in the racing form, you should first consider the races in which all the horses have run. Look to a horse that will win after moving up in class. And sometimes a horse might be entered into a race, lose, and then move down to a level and then finish with a better result.

Racing Style

The next thing I consider is how horses run a race *(Figure 8)*. Some like to immediately take the lead, and we categorize these as front-runners. I always have thought it is difficult to run wire-to-wire, as opposed to stalking the pack or staying close to the others. Many short races may favor front-runners because it will be tough to catch a horse on the lead with only a short distance to go. It reminds you of the old fable about the tortoise and the hare.

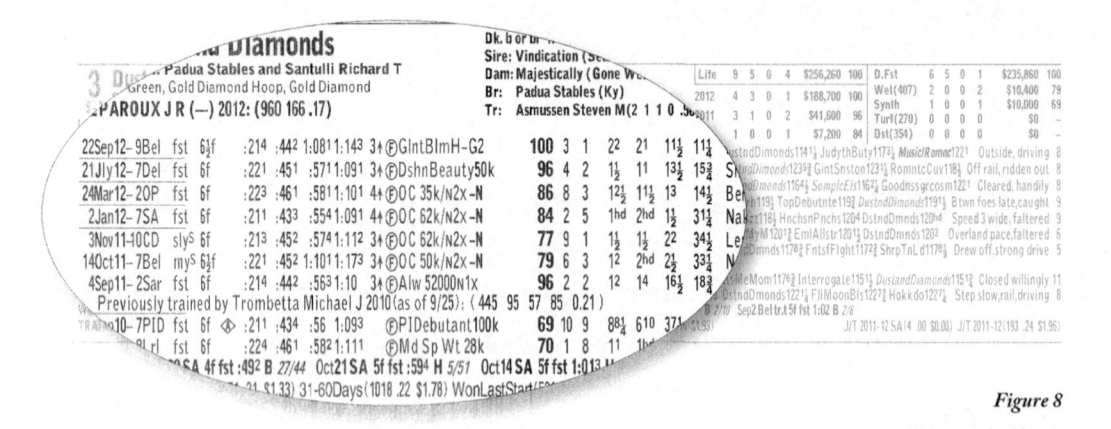

Figure 8

On the other hand, longer distances give a greater shot to those who race up close or from behind, conserving energy and letting the front-runners burn themselves out What you need to do is compare all the horses and see if there's one that may not have any competition on the front end. If you only have one or two front-running style horses, you may look to the front-runner to win or at least come in second or third. If it looks like there are a few that will battle each other, you may want to look to a stalker or closer that will push fast speed fractions and let the front-runners tire each other out. In either case, look at the pace of the race. History doesn't always repeat itself, but horses tend to like a certain running style and will most likely run their best races using that same style. In the case of 'Dust and Diamonds,' you can see she loves running in the front end and loves the shorter-distance races of 6 furlongs. Let's now look at time fractions from the past races of a horse.

Fractions

There are three areas we need to look at for 'Dust and Diamonds' ***(Figure 9)***. The first is the date and track the horse last raced. The second one is the fractions that were set by the leading horse, and the last one is where 'Dust and Diamonds' began the race and where she was during certain portions of the race. In this case, 'Dust and Diamonds' ran her last race on September 22, 2012, at Belmont at a distance of 6½ furlongs. The fractions show how fast the lead horse was running at that point of the race. 'Dust and Diamonds' came out of the 3rd gate position and jumped out to the lead, ran second for most of the race, was in first for the last portion and finished in first.

3 Dust and Diamonds

22Sep12-9Bel	fst	6½f	:21⁴	:44²	1:08¹	1:14³	3↑ⒻGlntBlmH-G2	**100**	3	1	2²	2¹	1¹½	1¹¼	Leparoux J R	L114
21Jly12-7Del	fst	6f	:22¹	:45¹	:57¹	1:09¹	3↑ⒻDshnBeauty50k	**96**	4	2	1½	1¹	1³½	1⁵¾	Smith M E	L123
24Mar12-2OP	fst	6f	:22³	:46¹	:58¹	1:10¹	4↑ⒻOC 35k/N2x -**N**	**86**	8	3	1²½	1¹½	1³	1⁴½	Berry M C	L116

1¹¼ Leparoux J R	L114	8.80	99- 10	DustndDimonds114¹¼ JudythButy117³¼ ***MusiclRomnc***122¹	Outside, driving 8
1⁵¾ Smith M E	L123	2.10	95- 14	*DustndDimonds*123⁵¾ GintSnston123¹¼ RomntcCuv118½	Off rail, ridden out 8
1⁴½ Berry M C	L116	*.80	91- 12	*DustndDmonds*116⁴½ *SomplcEls*116²¼ Goodnssgrcosm122¹	Cleared, handily 8

Figure 9

For this race, the fractions were 21-4/5 seconds for the first quarter-mile, 44-2/5 for the half-mile, 1:08-1/5 at 6 furlongs and finished the race in 1:14-3/5. That's really fast for a 6½ furlong race. You also can tell how many lengths the horse was behind the leader at each point of the race. 'Dust and Diamonds' was in second by 2 lengths, then second by 1 length, in first by 1½ and ended the same way, winning by 1½ lengths. In summary, these stats show me that this horse is a front-runner for most of her races, sets fast fractions for shorter distance races, has be ridden by the same jockey as her last win and has moved up in class and won. The next piece of the formula to consider is the Beyer Speed Figure.

Beyer Speed Figure

The Beyer Speed Figure is a system designed in the early 1970s by Andrew Beyer, a syndicated horse racing columnist for The Washington Post. It was formulated to rate the performances of thoroughbred racehorses in North America. This system is probably the most recognized and provides a statistic of how a horse performed against others. It evolved to measure each horse's performance, reflected by a number that can be compared as a speed figure.

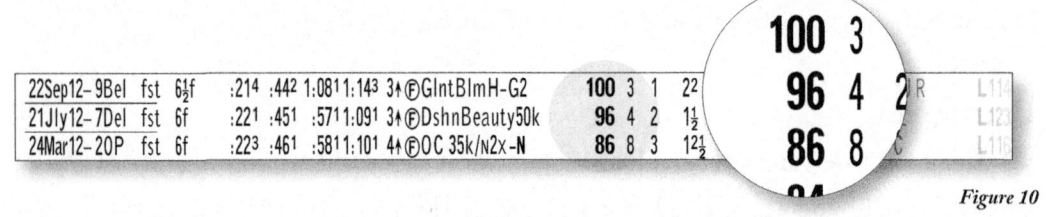

Figure 10

After each race, a number is assigned to the horse, taking into account each horse in that particular race *(Figure 10)*. Then, the horse's performance is compared to other tracks at similar distances and adjusted to reflect similar races. Thankfully, you don't need to know exactly how the numbers are computed, but you need to understand what they stand for. In theory, a horse with a higher Beyer Speed Figure should be faster than that of a lower-numbered horse. But you can't always use these to pick your winners. It should be used as a tool to identify horses that are better or worse than another. Many times it helps me make the final choice whether to choose that horse or another one.

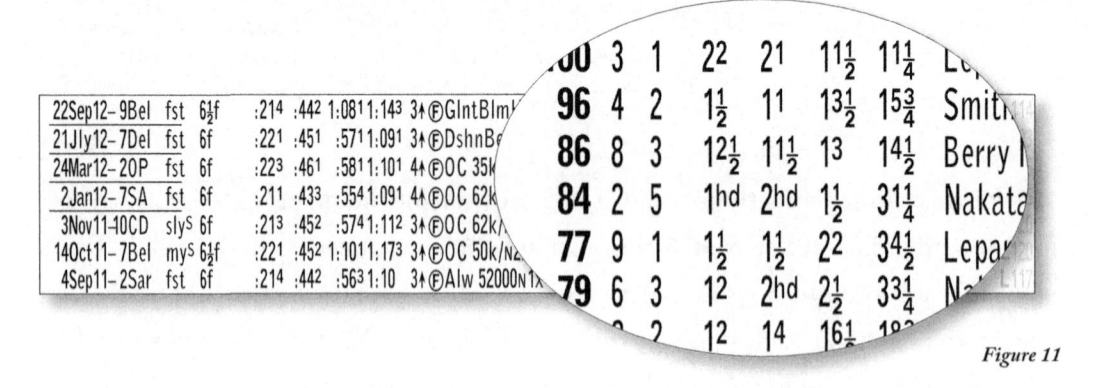

Figure 11

Following the actual race stats of what positions they ran, *Figure 11* highlights important information that may help you in deciding if this is one of your potential horses to include in your picks.

Jockey, Weight and Odds

The first name following the race stats is the jockey. In *Figure 12* you can see that Julian Leparoux rode this horse last time. Many times, horses run on some type of drug that is legal in the sport. When they do, it is listed as a single-letter abbreviation before the weight (L114). In this case, the drug is Lasix and the jockey carried a weight of 114 pounds. Lasix is a common drug used and allowed in racing. Lasix, technically furosemide, is used as a preventative treatment for 'Exercise-Induced Pulmonary Hemorrhage,' a very common occupational disease which affects the lungs of race horses. And you can see that 'Dust and Diamonds' not only will be running this race on Lasix, she has used the medication each of the nine times she has raced.

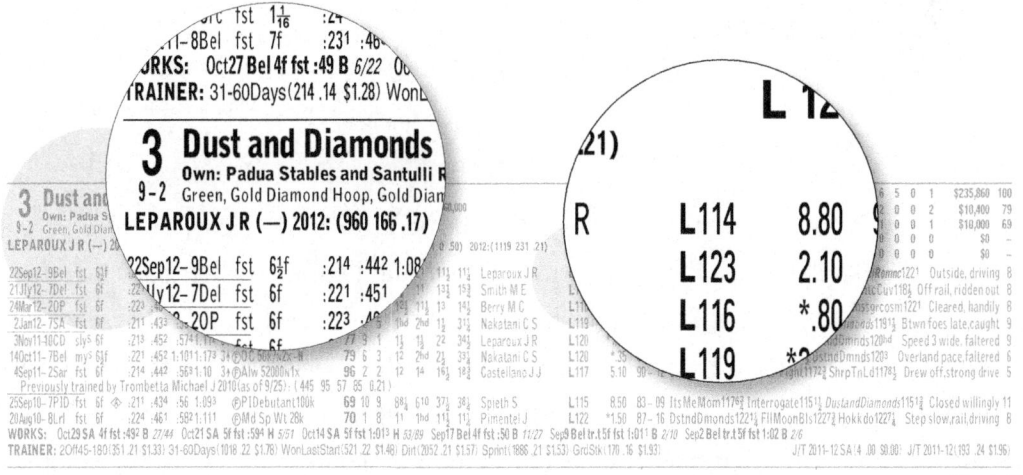

Figure 12

One important thing to notice is that the last time the horse ran, she carried 114 pounds and will now be carrying 124 pounds. That may make the difference between winning and losing. In racing, the amount of weight carried can be an equalizer. Many Stakes races dictate the amount of weight for each horse to be the same. This way it should look to be an equal race with no one horse having an advantage over another. While this information may seem simple, I always take note of how a horse does carrying a given weight. Remember, this is an equalizer. If the weight goes up significantly, your horse may have a tougher time running with the competition.

You may not always get the same jockey on the horse, as trainers and owners like to use those jockeys who have performed well for them. Like the saying goes, 'if it ain't broke, don't fix it.' And of course everyone wants to have the best jockeys riding their horses. Many times, a jockey will leave a horse ridden in the past and jump to

Smarter Bets – The Exacta Way

another horse that might have a better shot. If there's a situation where there are two horses you like and you notice the jockey has moved from one ridden in the past to another one in that race, it may be an indication of a better mount and possible win. Now, I am not saying that this is always the case, but I do think about this when looking at my competition. Why would you get off a horse you have done well with to ride another one? The likely answer is you think there's a better chance of winning on the new mount. I have seen this on numerous occasions and, more often than not, the horse that the jockey rides finishes ahead of the horse the jockey left. This is only my gut feeling. While I can't quantify the numbers, it is just what I have experienced and seen time and time again.

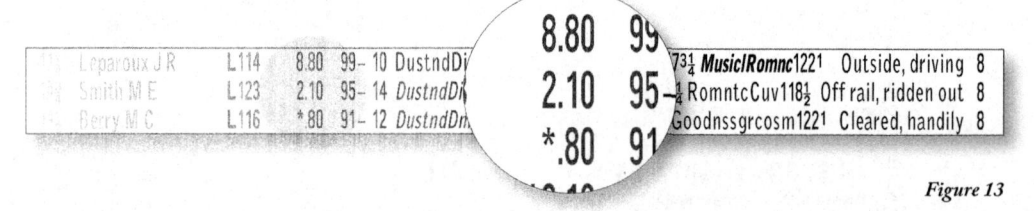

Figure 13

The next bit of information *(Figure 13)* is the odds for the horse when it last raced. You can see that in the last three races run by 'Dust and Diamonds,' her odds increased each time. On March 24th at Oaklawn Park (OP), she was the odds-on favorite at .80 to 1. The asterisk* in front of the .80 indicates that horse was the favorite in the race. She raced in an Optional Claiming race of non-winners of two races and won as the favorite. After that race she moved up to a $50,000 Stakes race and went off at the odds of $2.10-1 and also won that race. For the most recent race, 'Dust and Diamonds' went off at odds of $8.80-1 and also won that race. She improved not only her Beyer's figures but also paid off at higher odds, all while moving up in class. Now that's the kind of horse I like to bet on in a race!

Standard Speed Rating

The last items to look at are the numbers next to the line and the names and comments to the right. As you recall, the bold numbers located in the middle of the line indicate speed figures that compare each horse to all horses in the that type of race all across the country. But when you look at the two numbers after the weight the horse carries, that is a little different from the Beyer's numbers. This gives you a clue as to how a horse raced at that track for that particular race, and performance against the record time set for that race. Let's take a closer look at these numbers.

We want to look at the first number in the series 99-10. In the case of 'Dust and Diamonds,' her number was 99 *(Figure 14)*. What that means is that the horse ran 1/5 of a second slower than the track record for that particular race. That would seem pretty fast if it was the only number you looked at. But we also need to consider the second number, which is an average for all horses that day at that track as a relationship to the record time for this race.

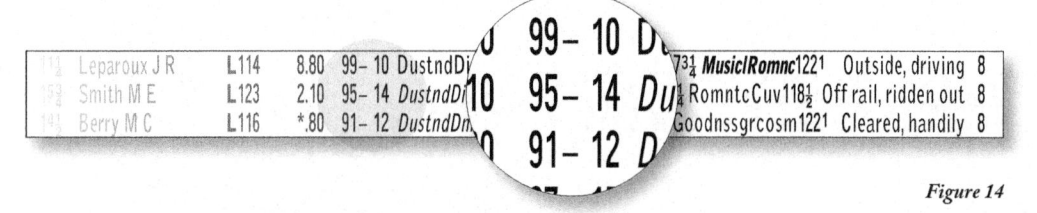

Figure 14

In the case of 'Dust and Diamonds,' horses that day all were given the equalizer number of 10. What I do is add the two numbers together to see how that horse compares to other horses that day. Based on this resulting number, the average of all the horses racing on September 22nd ran two seconds slower than the track record. That helps me when I compare the Beyer Speed Figure to every other horse in the race. In this case, I added 99 plus 10, equaling 109. The horse's Beyer Speed Figure in her last race was 100.

Now let's look at statistics on how 'Dust and Diamonds' has progressed up to this race. The secondary speed figures in both of her last races are the same (109), but were arrived at differently. In her last race, the first number was 99, and was 95 two races previously with only the second number differing. Since the Beyer's number increased while her secondary numbers remained the same, it shows how the horse has improved. Two races back, her Beyer Figure was 96, which is lower than her current 100. To me, this is a good indication a horse is improving. This might become an important factor while considering your potential horses.

I hope you paid attention to those last calculations. The Beyer Speed Figure is one of my more important aspects of handicapping. To me, a horse that runs consistently lower numbers against ones with higher numbers shows that the horse will have a much slimmer chance of winning. A horse that runs in the 60s shouldn't be expected to beat a horse that consistently runs in the 80s or 90s. I am not saying it can't happen, but what I am saying is that it isn't too probable. This is only one of the many handicapping skills I would like to share. Although I regard the Beyer Speed Figure an important part of my handicapping, it is not the final deciding factor that I use when comparing horses.

Comments

Let's take a closer look at a different race and the comments at the end of each line. Below is a DRF race entry for a horse named 'Win for Kitten.' This 3-year-old filly ran at Gulfstream Park on February 10, 2013. She was entered in a 1-1/16 mile $50,000 Optional Claiming race on turf with a purse of $36,300. I chose this horse because the comments from her last three races gave me valuable insight *(Figure 15)*.

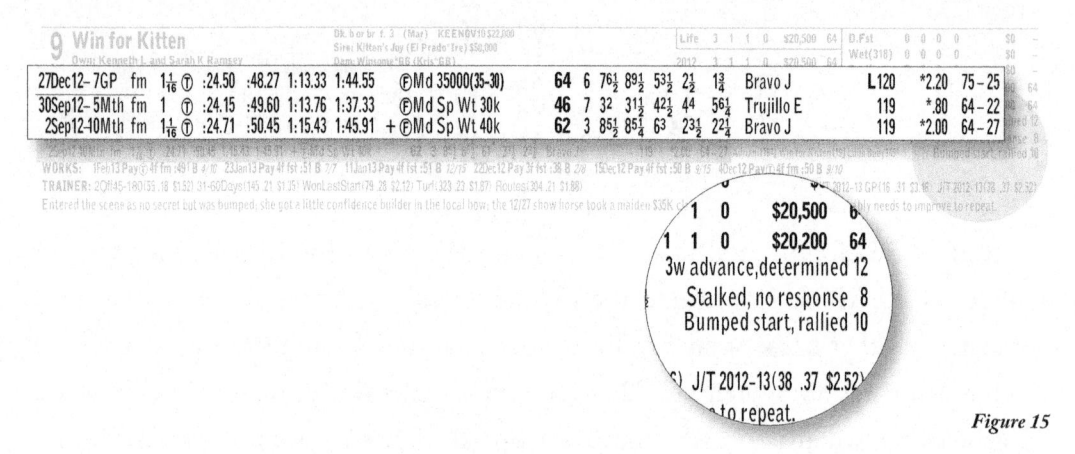

Figure 15

'Win for Kitten' was entered in a $40,000 Maiden race at Monmouth Park on September 2, 2012, and, according to the comments at the end of the line, was bumped in the start but rallied and came in second. That's a trait of a good horse. She overcame adversity and finished second, despite a troubled start. Her next race was 28 days later, also on Monmouth Park turf, but was entered in a Maiden race for a lower purse of $30,000, probably to gain a better advantage after her rocky start on September 2. In the notes, it shows that she stalked with no response. As you can see with her positions, she came out of the 7th post to start, ran in third and fourth most of the race and finished in 5th by 6¼ lengths. This wasn't a great race for 'Win for Kitten' and the comments really say it all. She had no response with 'E Trujillo' riding her. Following a three-month layoff, she went to Gulfstream Park in Florida and was entered in a Maiden race for $35,000. From the 6th post, she dropped to the back and ran 7th by 6½ lengths, 8th by 9½ lengths, 5th by 3½ lengths, 2nd by a 1/2-length and finished in first by ¾ of a length. The comment tells the tale. She went 3-wide around the others and was determined to win. With this information, I was convinced to include this horse in my exacta and place her on top. Other information I looked at which helped me in my determination was that she was using Lasix (L) for the first time. In addition to that, she went back to the distance of 1-1/16 miles after running in a 1-mile race on September 30 and performing well in her 1-1/16 mile race on September 2. And the kicker was a return to jockey Joe Bravo after doing nothing with Trujillo in her second race.

The last things I look at are the comments at the bottom of each horse's information. In this case, "Entered the scene as no secret but was bumped; she got a little confidence builder in the local bow; the 12/27 show horse took a Maiden $35K claimer here 1/25 with a 65 figure; probably needs to improve to repeat" solidified my thoughts exactly. As I stated before, we need to use all the tools to make the 'Smarter Bets – the Exacta Way' in order to make the most of our winnings.

Comments are important when determining whether a horse should be placed into your choices or not. You usually can tell why a horse wins a race, but many times I look for reasons why a horse loses. In many races, a horse may look like a standout but ends up faltering and placing 'out of the money.' That's when I look to the comments. We don't all watch every race or even keep up with them, but the comment section really helps you understand what happened in a race, and why.

The next page *(Figure 16)* shows the results from that 1-1/6 mile race at Gulfstream Park. It shows that 'Win for Kitten' raced well from behind the pack, just like she did in her previous wins. She closed and ran down a 13-1 shot to win by a ½-length, ridden by Joe Bravo. She improved off her last race and earned $17,400 for first place. Her winning time for the race was 1:43-1/5, which is shown above the payouts. The time fractions of the lead horse at specific portions of the race show the first ¼-mile was run in 23-3/5 seconds, the half-mile in 47-3/5 seconds, three-quarters of a mile in 1:12-4/5 (all set by 'Peekytoes'), the stretch was hit in 1:37 flat ('Swear Me In') and that 'Win the Kitten' finished the race with a time of 1:43-1/5.

Overall Perception

Considering all these factors and also using the Daily Racing Form helps me determine what horses to include in my exacta picks. I look at all pieces of information and utilize that data to choose the best horses in order to maximize my wagers.

You won't be able to find all this information in other publications. It's important to find the needle in the haystack and, in my expert opinion, the best resource with which to do that is the DRF.

Smarter Bets – The Exacta Way

SEVENTH RACE
Gulfstream
FEBRUARY 10, 2013

1 1/16 MILES. (Turf) (1.38) STARTER OPTIONAL CLAIMING. Purse $36,300 (includes $7,300 FOA – Florida Owners Awards) FOR FILLIES THREE YEARS OLD WHICH HAVE STARTED FOR A CLAIMING PRICE OF $50,000 OR LESS AND WHICH HAVE NEVER WON A RACE OTHER THAN MAIDEN OR CLAIMING OR OPTIONAL CLAIMING PRICE $50,000. Weight, 122 lbs. Non-winners of a race at a mile or over since January 10 Allowed 2 lbs. Such a race since December 10, 2012 Allowed 4 lbs. Claiming Price $50,000 (Races Where Entered For $30,000 Or Less Not Considered) (Condition Eligibility). (If deemed inadvisable to run this race over the turf course, it will be run on the main track at One Mile and One Sixteenth) (Rail at 108 feet).

Value of Race: $29,000 Winner $17,400; second $5,800; third $2,610; fourth $1,160; fifth $290; sixth $290; seventh $290; eighth $290; ninth $290; tenth $290; eleventh $290. Mutuel Pool $361,920.00 Exacta Pool $295,734.00 Trifecta Pool $172,864.00 Superfecta Pool $116,111.00

Last Raced	Horse	M/Eqt.	A.	Wt	PP	St	1/4	1/2	3/4	Str	Fin	Jockey	Cl'g Pr	Odds $1
27Dec12 7GP1	Win for Kitten	L	3	120	9	4	9½	91	9½	31	1½	Bravo J		5.10
1Dec12 5Tam1	Swear Me In	L	3	118	8	10	3½	3hd	2½	1½	2no	Trujillo E		13.10
3Jan13 9GP5	In Haste	L	3	118	2	9	10 4½	105	8½	4½	3½	Lanerie C J		5.20
16Jan13 5GP2	I Know It All	L	3	118	1	7	5½	4½	31	2½	4 1½	Velazquez J R		3.00
16Jan13 5GP1	Rhythm Queen	L b	3	122	4	8	7½	81	102	7 1½	5nk	Rocco J S Jr	50000	3.60
16Jan13 5GP5	Sharapova Slams	L b	3	120	5	1	4 1½	52	4½	51	6 1½	Prado E S		8.60
13Jan13 11GP1	Fly Gal	L b	3	122	11	11	8½	7½	5½	6½	72	Husbands P		13.90
10Jan13 5GP4	Dolly Double	L	3	118	10	3	6 1	6½	6½	8 1½	84	Rosario J		39.10
30Jan13 2GP4	Royal Geisha	L bf	3	118	6	5	11	11	11	11	9 3¼	Lopez P		38.90
30Dec12 2GP1	Peekytoes	L b	3	118	3	2	15	14	1hd	93	10 2¾	Cruz M R		22.90
16Jan13 5GP3	Iwillneversaynever	L	3	118	7	6	2 1½	2½	7hd	101	11	Saez L		10.90

OFF AT 3:40 Start Good. Won driving. Course firm.
TIME :23³, :47⁴, 1:12⁴, 1:37, 1:43¹ (:23.65, :47.75, 1:12.80, 1:37.11, 1:43.31)

$2 Mutuel Prices:

9 –WIN FOR KITTEN	12.20	6.60	4.80
8 –SWEAR ME IN		12.40	6.80
2 –IN HASTE			5.40

$2 EXACTA 9–8 PAID $173.00 $1 TRIFECTA 9–8–2 PAID $846.70
$1 SUPERFECTA 9–8–2–1 PAID $4,387.00

Dk. b or br. f, (Mar), by Kitten's Joy – Winsome–GB, by Kris–GB. Trainer Clement Christophe. Bred by Royal Oak Farm LLC Kenneth L Ramsey & Sarah K Ramsey (Ky).

WIN FOR KITTEN outrun early, swung wide for the stretch run, then rallied to be up in time. SWEAR ME IN tracked the pace, rallied to take over on the far turn, made the pace to deep stretch but couldn't resist the winner while just saving the place. IN HASTE unhurried early, saved ground and rallied to just miss the place. I KNOW IT ALL reserved off the pace, rallied three wide around the far turn to reach near even terms for command, tried the leaders to deep stretch and weakened. RHYTHM QUEEN allowed to settle, closed with a belated rally without threatening. SHARAPOVA SLAMS rated off the pace, advanced along the inside to loom a threat on the far turn, then gave way. FLY GAL off slowly, circled rivals four wide around the far turn to reach contention, then tired. DOLLY DOUBLE raced three wide and faltered. ROYAL GEISHA was outrun. PEEKYTOES sprinted to a clear lead along the inside, made the pace into the far turn, then had nothing left. IWILLNEVERSAYNEVER chased the pace off the rail into the far turn and faded.

Owners– 1, Ramsey Kenneth L and Sarah K; 2, Goodwood Racing II; 3, Bottom Line Racing Stable and Rebel Tide Racing LLC; 4, Champion Equine LLC; 5, Calabrese Frank C; 6, Mighty White Stallion LLC; 7, Oxley John C; 8, Red Oak Stable (Brunetti); 9, Saiden Amin; 10, Kerr George J; 11, Jacobson Rachel and Auricchio Dominick

Trainers– 1, Clement Christophe; 2, Cibelli Jane; 3, Proctor Thomas F; 4, Braddy J David; 5, Ramirez Luis M; 6, Sano Antonio; 7, Casse Mark; 8, Sacco Gregory D; 9, Sano Antonio; 10, Braddy J David; 11, Fawkes David

$2 Daily Double (9–9) Paid $215.00 ; Daily Double Pool $37,503.
$1 Pick Three (8–9–9) Paid $291.90 ; Pick Three Pool $46,477.

Copyright © 2013 Daily Racing Form, Inc. and Equibase Company, all rights reserved

Data provided or compiled by Daily Racing Form, Inc. and Equibase Company generally are accurate but occasionally errors and omissions occur as a result of incorrect data received from others, mistakes in processing and other causes. Daily Racing Form, Inc. and Equibase Company disclaim responsibility for the consequences, if any, of such errors, but would appreciate their being called to their attention.

Figure 16

Keith Hoffman *'The Derbyman'*

CHAPTER 8

CLASS, PACE AND HOW THEY RACE

28Dec12–3GP	fm	5f	Ⓣ	:21.75	:44.12	:56.29	3↑ Clm 25000(25–20)	
13Dec12–8GP	fm	5f	Ⓣ	:21.49	:44.55	:56.29	3↑ OC 25k/N1x	

Previously trained by Tom Dascombe

Gulfstream Park 1⅛ MILES

5 FOA - Florida Owners Awards) For Four Year Olds
mile or over since January 10 Allowed 2 lbs. Such a ra
$40,000 (Rail at 48 feet).

$1 Bet 3 — Beyer par: 91

Life	28	4	1	3	$52,989	66	D.Fst	0 0 0 0	$0	–
2012	14	3	0	2	$21,880	66	Wet(380)	0 0 0 0	$0	–
2011	9	0	1	0	$5,154	–	Synth	4 0 0 2	$1,472	–
GP Ⓣ	2	0	0	0	$695	66	Turf(359*)	24 4 1 1	$51,517	66
							Dst Ⓣ(224)	0 0 0 0	$0	–

Post time: 2:37 ET — Wagers: $1 Daily Double, $1 Exacta, $.50 Trifecta, $.10 Superfecta, $1 Bet 3 — Beyer par: 91

1 Julius Geezer (Ire) B. g. 5 (Apr)
Own: Wildcard Racing Syndicate Sire: Antonius Pius (Danzig) $40,000
20–5 Nvy, Pink Dots, Pink Sleeves, Pink Cap Dam: Victoria's Secret*Ire (Law Society)
$40,000 Br: Ballyhane Stud (Ire)
LANERIE C J (171 16 18 14 .09) 2012: (1111 20

L 119

28Dec12–3GP	fm	5f Ⓣ :21.75 :44.12	:56.29	3↑ Clm 25000(25–20)	**51**	3 6	9 4¾ 10 7¼ 9 8½ 9 9¼
13Dec12–8GP	fm	5f Ⓣ :21.49 :44.55	:56.29	3↑ OC 25k/N1x	**66**	5 7	8⁵ 7⁶ 8 5¾ 5 5¾

Previously trained by Tom Dascombe

8Nov12	Wolverhampton (GB) ft	6f ◊LH	1:13⁴	3↑ 32redbet.com Claiming Stakes		3¹
	Racing Post Rating: 88			W c 4000		
20Oct12	Wolverhampton (GB) ft	5f ◊LH	1:01¹	3↑ Foley Steels Claiming Stakes		7⁸
	Racing Post Rating: 57			W c 5100		
7Sep12	Haydock (GB) gf	6f Ⓣ Str	1:12²	3↑ Betfred Handicap Stakes (Div I)		12⁵
	Racing Post Rating: 74			Hcp 10400		
24Aug12	Newmarket (GB) gf	6f Ⓣ Str	1:12¹	3↑ Piper-Heidsieck Handicap Stakes		6 4¼
	Racing Post Rating: 82			Hcp 12700		
9Aug12	Haydock (GB) gd	6f Ⓣ Str	1:13⁴	3↑ Pro Footballers Assoc TRC H'cap Stks (Div II)		4 3¼
	Racing Post Rating: 85			Hcp 10200		
27Jly12	York (GB) gf	6f Ⓣ Str	1:11²	4↑ Seddon Property Services Stakes		1no
	Racing Post Rating: 89			Hcp 12600		
20Jun12	Hamilton (GB) gd	6f Ⓣ Str	1:10³	3↑ Sam Collingwood-Cameron Handicap Stakes		4 4½
	Racing Post Rating: 78			Hcp 7900		
13Jun12	Hamilton (GB) gd	6f Ⓣ Str	1:10	4↑ Handicap Stakes		1 1¾
	Racing Post Rating: 85			Hcp 12500		

WORKS: 24Jan13 PmM 4f fst :48² B 9/21 9Dec12 PmM 3f fst :38⁴ B 1/3
TRAINER: Sprint/Route(1.00 $0.00) 31-60Days(1.00 $0.00) Turf(4.00

Figure 17

37

Smarter Bets – The Exacta Way

In this chapter, I want you to look at a race and actually pick the horses you might include in bets. First, I will show you the actual race information as seen in the DRF (Daily Racing Form) which, as I mentioned previously, you can purchase either online at www.drf.com or at a racetrack, newsstand or off-track betting location.

We will handicap a Claiming race for $40,000, run on turf at the distance of 1-1/8 miles. It is for 4-year-olds and older, with horses and jockeys carrying 123 pounds. Non-winners of a race at a mile or over since January 10th are allowed to take off 2 pounds, and a race since December 10, 2012, will get a 4-pound allowance. If horses meet these qualifications, they can get a reduction in weight and potentially an edge on the others in the race. *(Figure 17 on previous page.)*

The first thing to look at in *Figure 17* is the type of race (Stakes, Claiming, etc.). This horse is a 5-year-old gelding that raced in Europe prior to his two races in the United States, six and eight weeks prior to this one. It looks like he was racing for smaller Stakes races before retreating to Claiming races. In 2012, 'Julius Geezer' raced 14 times, had 3 wins and 2 third-place finishes but only won $21,880. His lifetime best Beyer Speed Figure is 66 and is shown in the boldface next to his lifetime stats. We will use this number to compare his stats to the rest of the field. As we will see, the horse in this race with the best Beyer Figure had a 91. 'Julius Geezer' mostly ran 6-furlong races (3/4-mile) prior to today's 1-1/8 mile run. Looking at the pace, we can't really see how he did in Europe so we need to look at the comments section on the right side of the DRF entry. This information is valuable because we weren't there. Since coming to the United States, 'Julius Geezer' ran in a $25,000 Optional Claiming race on turf, for non-winners of one race, at a 5-furlong distance (a short 5/8-mile) and then another 5-furlong $25,000 Claiming race, in both of which he finished poorly, in fifth and ninth place, respectively. And now we see the horse moving up in class to a $40,000 Claiming race at a much longer distance (8½ furlongs instead of 5). His workouts are marginal and show only one workout since his last race at a distance of 4 furlongs, on January 24th. Although his time was 48-2/5 seconds, he was 9th of 21 horses training that day at that distance. I would prefer to have seen at least a 5-furlong or mile workout to prep for his longer upcoming race. Based on these factors, I will take him out of my selections. Now let's take a look at the 2 and 3 horses *(Figure 18)*.

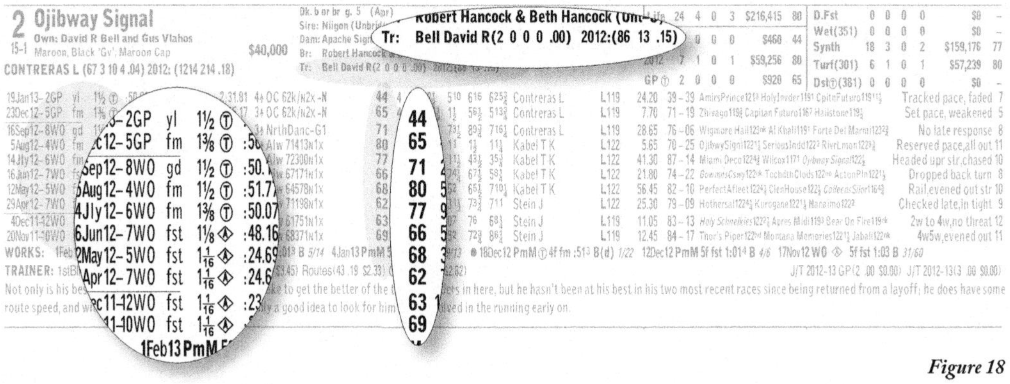

Figure 18

There are a number of indicators that lead me not bet on the 2 horse. It's good to see stats that a horse already has raced the same distance of the one in which he's now entered. Of course, you can't always find a horse that has done this because he always has to have a first race at a given distance. But since there are others who have raced the distance and have good Beyer Speed Figures, I am not yet convinced my logic is not valid. The one thing we can say about 'Ojibway Signal' is that he already raced at higher race levels but, unfortunately, didn't do very well. His Beyer Speed Figures for the past few races were an unimpressive 44 and 65, even though both races were Optional Claiming for non-winners of two races, at a level of $62,000. I did notice, however, that his last race was on a 'yielding' track, so I think I'd throw out that race and not put much emphasis on it. Looking at the trainer's stats, he had an unimpressive 15-percent win total in 2012 (13 of 86 races). This is shown next to the notes of trainer David Bell (Tr: Bell David). His 2012 racing career, with the exception of the December 23 race at Gulfstream Park, was in Canada at Woodbine. Considering all these factors, I will look elsewhere for a contender.

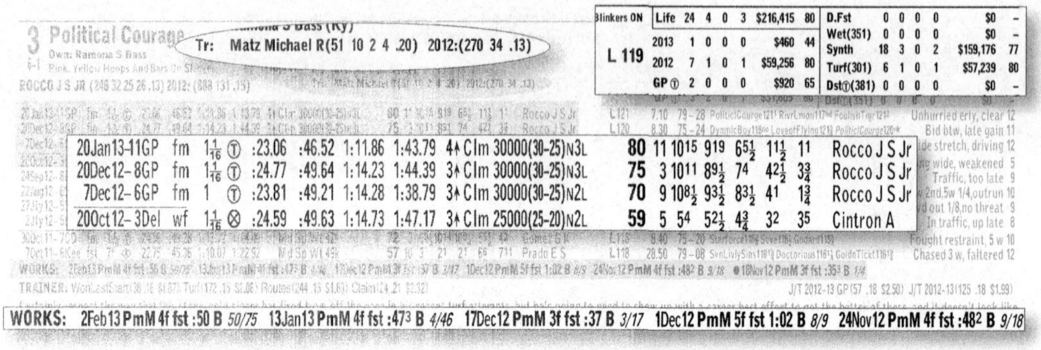

Smarter Bets – The Exacta Way

Figure 19

A more intriguing horse is #3, 'Political Courage' *(Figure 19)*. Stepping up in class from the $30,000 Claiming ranks, he now tries as a 4-year-old in a little tougher group ($40,000) after a solid win at just a little shorter distance than today. His lifetime record at Gulfstream Park on turf shows 2 wins and 1 third, out of three races. I love to see a horse that does well at a particular track. When they get comfortable and like the surface and feel of a track, they tend to perform better. Think about it. When you drive to work, you probably take the same route each day. The ease and comfort of the familiarity makes things easier for you, just as if a horse ran the same distance consistently at his home course.

The trainer is a good one. Not only is Michael Matz a seasoned trainer in thoroughbred racing, but he was an American Olympic equestrian team member inducted into the show jumping Hall of Fame. Matz was a six-time U.S. national champion and won at least one major show jumping event in 20 consecutive years! But when it comes to horse racing, his credits are equally impressive. A few of his most noted winners were 2003 Florida and Kentucky Derby winner 'Barbaro,' 2006 Breeder's Cup Distaff winner 'Round Pond' and 2012 Belmont Stakes winner and 2012 Breeder's Cup Juvenile race 2nd place finisher 'Union Rags.' With these credentials, it is a must to consider his horses as competitors. But you can't just rely on the trainer --you also must look at the horse.

'Political Courage' shows me encouragement with Beyer figures increasing in each of his last three races, which shows improvement. His workout times also are important. I like that prior to his December 20th race, he worked 3 furlongs on December 12th in: 37 flat and was third-fastest of 17 horses at that work distance. His next work was on January 13th in: 47-3/5, which was 4th of 46 horses and followed

40

by a win at the same $30,000 level as his previous race. But the one stat I don't like is his latest work on February 2nd, 4 furlongs in 50 seconds and 50th of 75 horses. That indicates to me he isn't ready for this level of race. Now I will be the first to say that all horse workouts are not the same. But if I see a pattern of workouts that turns into results, I won't count on that horse to perform to his best ability if his workouts do not show the same positive pattern for an upcoming race. His record on turf is good, with a Beyer Speed Figure of 80 and 3 wins, 1 second and 1 third in eight races. Taking all this into consideration, the 3 horse is in my mix of contenders.

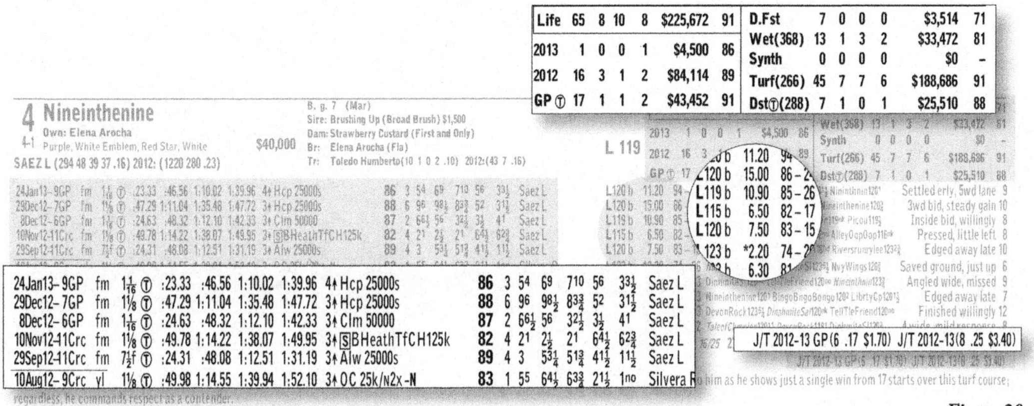

Figure 20

The 4 horse, 'Nineinthenine,' looks interesting *(Figure 20)*. The first thing I noticed is that his best Beyer Speed Figure of 91 came at Gulfstream (GP) on turf. He has raced 17 times on turf at Gulfstream with a mediocre record of 1 win, 1 second and 2 thirds, and earning $43,452 in winnings. The next thing I like about this horse is his 88 Beyer's Speed Rating at this distance. This is shown in Figure 19, under distance [Dist(t)]. It is marginal, but does show 1 win and 1 third 'in the money,' out of seven races. What impresses me about this horse is that his ratings over the past three races were consistent at 87, 88 and 86. I also like the fact that he has closed on the field in each of those races, finishing third twice and fourth once. And the fourth came in a higher $50,000 Claiming level. But the most impressive piece of information I took away from this horse is the speed ratings from these three races (94-17, 86-24 and 85-26). If you remember from a previous chapter, you should take note of how fast the horse ran, compared to other horses that raced that day. I add those numbers together to give me an idea of how good they are. Adding the numbers together show 111, 101 and 111, which are much higher than most of the others in this race. In addition, it shows that the jockey/trainer combination in 2012 has 25-percent wins. All of this is a plus, so I will add the 4 horse to the mix of potential horses.

After a 7½-furlong turf race on December 5th, 5 horse 'Clement Rock' was entered in a turf run of 1-1/8 mile (9 furlongs), a distance he had tried only three times out of his 11 lifetime races *(Figure 21)*. And out of these 11 lifetime races, he finished first five times and earned almost $250,000. As a 5-year-old, this tells me that he is a very good horse. This will be his third race since a four-month layoff. Additionally, in 2011, he won four of seven starts for $227,000.

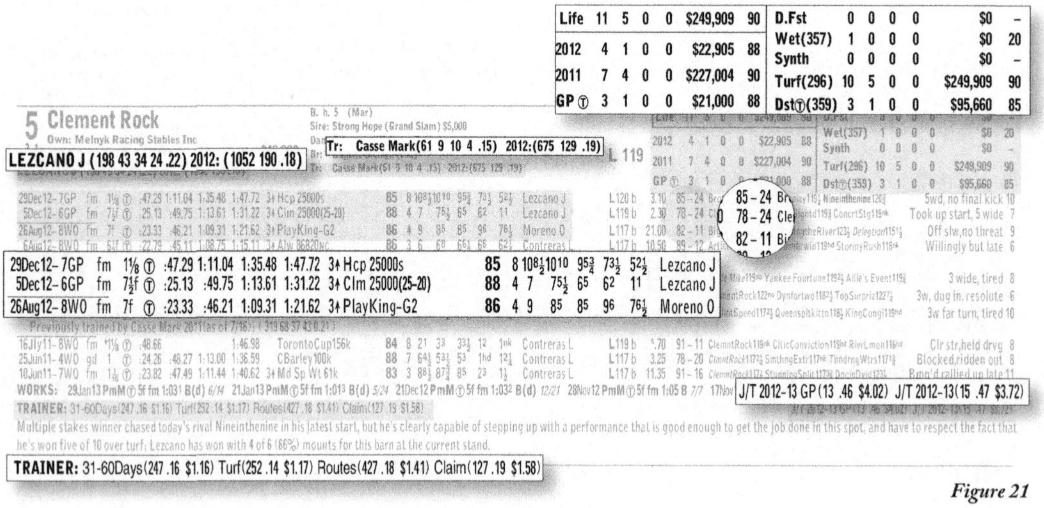

Figure 21

'Clement Rock' closed well in his last two starts and rated 88 and 85 Beyer Speed Figures since his short layoff. Also, trainer Mark Casse has a fantastic jockey/trainer win percentage [J/T 2012-13 GP (13 .46 $4.02)]

'Clement Rock' shows that he can compete in higher-class races and also has top Gulfstream jockey J. Lezcano aboard. His stats show a great 22-percent wins for Gulfstream rides in 2012 and 18-percent wins out of 1,052 rides for the entire year. This is important when looking at potential contenders. 'Clement Rock' has improved with his speed ratings, from 78 to 85, with the same 24 equalizer number. Adding the 85 to the 24 gives him a strong 109 figure, which compares closely to the 111 of #4 horse 'Nineinthenine.' The trainer shows stats of 16-percent winners with horses that have been laid off from 31-60 days. With all these positive indicators, I will include this contender among my choices.

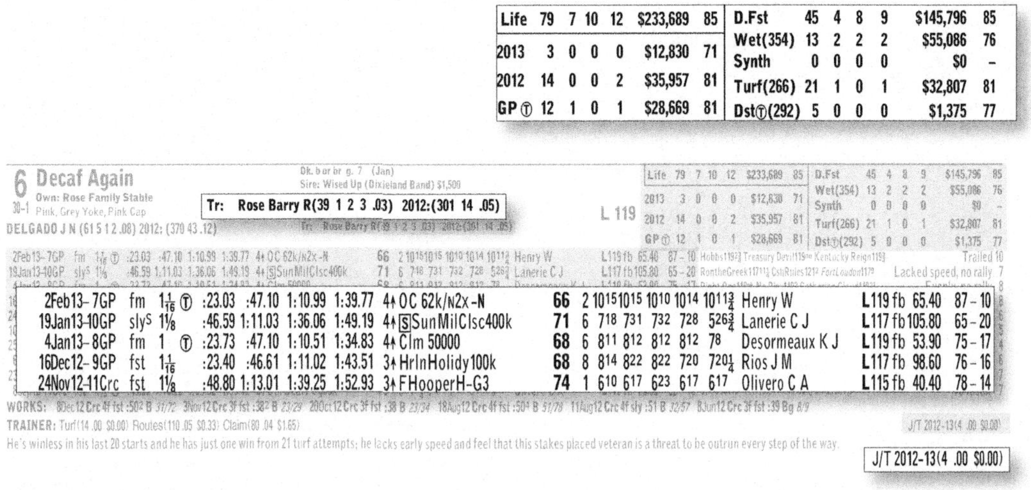

Keith Hoffman *'The Derbyman'*

Figure 22

There is nothing to like about the #6 horse, 'Decaf Again' *(Figure 22)*. He has low Beyer numbers (66, 71, 68, 68) in his last four races, has raced five times at this distance with no finishes in the money and his trainer and jockey are low-percentage winners. The horse's Beyer Speed Figure at this distance is 77, which is not very competitive, especially for this race. In seven years, this gelding has raced 79 times, winning almost 9-percent of his races. That isn't too impressive. If you look at all the comments following his races, the horse probably needs to be entered in lower-class competition. However, it looks like he has been entered in higher-purse races, which are not where he belongs. His turf record isn't strong, compared to his dirt races. On dirt, he has been in the money 21 out of 45 races, for about $146,000 in winnings. Based on these factors, I do not consider him a contender.

Let's next consider number 7, 'Minnie Punt' *(Figure 23 on the next page)*. There are a few things here that indicate he may be a contender and should be included in my exacta wagering. One of the first things to notice in the comments at the bottom is that this horse is a multiple Stakes winner that is rounding into form at lower levels.

43

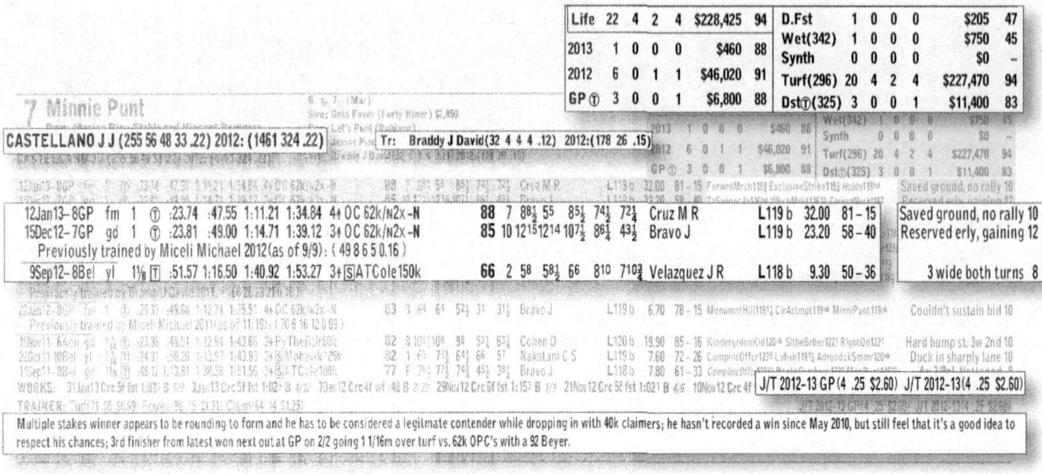

Smarter Bets – The Exacta Way

[Figure 23: Past performance chart for horse "7 Minnie Punt" with jockey Castellano J J and trainer Braddy J David]

Figure 23

As many handicappers do with diligence, I now look at the Beyer Speed Figures. The last two races for 'Minnie Punt' were 88 and 85, both at a mile on the turf. With this race being his third following a three-month layoff, it leads me to believe he should improve over his two most recent races, as many horses do. With both of these races being run at a mile on turf, this may be the one where he gets back to a better form and does well at the 1-1/16 mile distance. Handicappers must consider all racing angles to help us in our picks. Following a layoff, a horse needs a 'comeback race' that is comfortable. Here's a comparison. Have you ever tried something for the first time and felt like you weren't entirely ready for it, feeling like you need more practice, then the second and third time you gradually feel more comfortable doing it? That's also what it's like for a horses. They train for the race and need to feel comfortable in order to win. Some of my friends run marathons. They all train by running different distances in order to be at their peak performance for the big race. If they went out and ran their marathon without working up to it, they would be very disappointed with their results.

I like the Beyer Speed Figures this horse shows. If you look at his last two races, his numbers are 88 and 85, both improvements since his layoff. Although the 66 speed figure just prior to his layoff is very low, it was run on a yielding Belmont track in a $150,000 Stakes race, factors that I will disregard in my betting considerations unless the conditions on race day are the same. 'Minnie Punt' just doesn't like soft, wet turf. If you look at the August 12th race, he had a strong 91 Beyer Speed Figure in another $150,000 race. I like what I see from this 7-year-old gelding.

The next thing I notice is that this horse has been trained by the same two trainers. While at Belmont and Aqueduct in New York, the trainer was Michael Miceli. The trainer is David Braady when he runs at Gulfstream Park in Florida. Both trainers are comfortable and know which races to enter the horse. But 'familiarity breeds contempt,' as the saying goes. Three races at Gulfstream were run at the level of 'OC 62k/n2x-N,' or Optional Claiming Non-winners of two races at a claiming price of $62,000. He has been competitive at those levels, with his Beyer figures improving each time. Now he is running at a lower level of $40,000, which should make it an easier race than the last three at Gulfstream.

As I mentioned before, I like horses that are closers. Closers are horses running from behind the pack, saving their energy and using their bursts of speed towards the end of the race. In the case of 'Minnie Punt,' many of his races show that tendency. In his last race, he ran 7th and 8th most of the race but finished 2½ lengths back. In the race before that, on December 12th, he came from way back to finish 4th, only 3½ lengths back. To me, this shows he might be a better fit and a winner in a longer-distance race.

Jockeys are important to every good win. Some of them have better instincts than others. And more often than not, a great jockey can make the difference between a horse winning or finishing out of the money. J.J. Castellano is a very strong jockey. His stats show that he is winning 22-percent of his mounts this year at Gulfstream and also won 22-percent of his wins in 2012. Another important number I like to see is the percent of his mounts that are in the money. Don't forget that we are looking not only for horses that will win, but those to include in our exactas. In Castellano's case, he has been in the money almost 54-percent of the time. The entry: CASTELLANO J J (255 56 48 33 .22) shows that out of 255 races, he won 56 of them, came in second 48 times and third 33 times. If you add those three numbers and divide by the total amount of races (255) you will get 53.7-percent in the money. Not a bad horse to include in our exacta wagering!

With all this in mind, I like many of the things I see with 'Minnie Punt.' Let's keep looking at contenders, narrow it down to the top three and then we can make a well-educated bet.

Smarter Bets – The Exacta Way

Let's now look at the 8 horse, 'Dark Cove' *(Figure 24)*. I like what I see in the comments. His last race followed an 8-month layoff and was at Fair Grounds Race Course in New Orleans at a mile-and-1/16. Looking back in his races in 2011, he was a Stakes horse that raced at higher levels than today. Since we can't tell how every horse did in every race, the comment stating that the third-place finisher won his next race is important to know (the name of the horse –'Prime Cut'– is in italics). Typically, when a horse finishes just behind the winner, my handicapper's instinct tells me that he has a good chance of having a strong performance in his next race. Brian Pochman's comment at the bottom of the page regarding jockey 'Rosario' winning 36-percent for this barn will make me think twice about including this horse.

J/T 2012 -13 GP (14 .36 $2.37). This shows that in 2012, the jockey and trainer had 14 races together with 36-percent wins and a return on investment (ROI) of $2.37. This tells me that when he wins, it is most likely going to be at low odds which aren't always bad. Remember, we are looking for horses to include in our exacta wagering.

Figure 24

The trainer, Michael Maker, shows outstanding statistics: Maker Michael J (55 15 6 8 .27) 2012 (737 159 .22). In 55 races this year, Maker has had 15 winners, or 27-percent of his starters. When I add the 15, 6 and 8 together for 29 horses in the money and then divide by the total amount of races (55), it gives me about 53-percent in the money. And with 2012 stats showing 22-percent winners, I think the stats on this trainer are a plus.

The speed figures are extremely important in horse racing. 'Dark Cove' had taken some time off from April 26, 2012, until his next race on January 5th. And as I mentioned earlier, it may be tough for a horse to come back from a long layoff and be ready to race. Now, I am not saying you can't win a race following a layoff, but many trainers condition horses and need one or two races before they are in a good position to win. I like what I see in the following two statistics: 2off180 (12 .17 $0.88) and 31-60days (312 .24 $1.73). Maker's history shows that 24-percent of his horses return from 31-60 days layoff with a win. Those are impressive stats. Now when you combine that with the fact that 17-percent are winners of their second race off 180 days, both these stats stand out to me as a big plus for a contender. Not only does 'Dark Cove' fall into those statistical opportunities, he returned from that long layoff with a fantastic speed figure of 85. For a horse to do that after that long layoff means to me that he is in shape and ready to run.

Speed figures are always a very important indicator to consider. After primarily racing in Stakes races in 2011, 'Dark Cove' moved up nicely to Allowance races in 2012. The competition he faced in Stakes races in 2011 proved a little too strong compared to the level this horse should have been racing. Although he raced four times and only finished that year with one win, his Beyer's figures were good. In his first start after a 6-month layoff, he returned with a win and a strong speed figure of 88, followed by three additional races with speed figures of 86, 91 and 58. Of those speed figures, the impressive 91 in his third race after the layoff is the number that sticks in my mind. That was run on turf and fits well with his strong ability to win.

'Dark Cove' runs better on turf than on dirt. By checking out his Beyer Speed Figures in the top right-hand part of the stats information, it shows he has run three times on dirt with no wins and an 85 speed figure. Compare that to his turf races: 10 races with 3 wins, 1 second and 1 third, earnings of almost $139,000 and a highest speed figure of 95. That is a sure indicator that this horse should be running on turf to offer the best opportunity to win.

Another tidbit of information that is a hidden gem in the form is that 'Dark Cove' was claimed in his last race. That information jumps out, at first glance. But the hidden gem to note is that he was claimed at the end of the racing meet at Keeneland.

Smarter Bets – The Exacta Way

Keeneland is a premier racetrack in Lexington, Kentucky, that runs two short meets, in April and then again in October. They tend to race some of the best horses in the country and then see them depart for other tracks to continue their racing careers. New owners Kenneth and Sarah Ramsey, who are well-known in many Kentucky racing arenas, have purchased many successful horses, especially turf horses.

The Ramseys purchased their horse farm in 1994 from Almahurst Farms before changing the name to Ramsey Farms. Natives of Artemus, in eastern Kentucky, Kenneth sold his business of cellular telephone network franchises for $39 million and then decided to invest in his hobby of horse racing. As Eclipse winners in 2004 for Outstanding Owners, the Ramseys have had great horses like turf champions 'Kitten's Joy' and Grade 1 winner 'Roses in May,' winner of the 2005 Dubai World Cup, along with 'Precious Kitten' who was named a finalist for the 2008 Eclipse Award for Champion Female Turf Horse. Considering the long and impressive history of turf horses in their barn, you can see why the Ramseys purchase of 'Dark Cove' is worth noting.

The claiming information shows that the Ramsey's purchased the horse from "Englehart Joseph, Magdalena Racing and Trussell Robert for $50,000 [McPeek Kenneth 2012 (as of 4/26): (156 25 25 16 0.16)]." Kenny McPeek trained 156 horses this year, of which 25 won, 25 came in second and 16 came in third, for 16-percent winners. If you added his money winners of 25, 25 and 16 and then divided that by 156, you come out with 41-percent of his starters to date are in the money.

Magdalena Farm is owned and operated by Kenny McPeek. He trains and ships horses all over the country to compete with the best. So as we look at horses and where they came from, be sure to do a little homework ahead of time if you want to gain insight and help with your exacta winners. For many of you, it will be easier to look at the stats and keep in mind the tidbits of information you gain from watching each race.

Jockeys, as the rider of the horse, can make the difference between winning and losing. With Joel Rosario in the saddle, the form shows a 'rider switch' to a talented jockey. His stats: Rosario J (229 47 39 35 .21) 2012 (1216 232 .19) tell us that 21-percent of his starts at Gulfstream were winners. If you add 47, 35 and 35 and divide them by 229, it shows you 51-percent in the money results. Changing from a good turf jockey like Leparoux to Joel Rosario shows me that the Ramsey's and new trainer Michael Maker are doing everything possible to improve their chances of winning with this horse. With all this information, I am making 'Dark Cove' my top choice to include in my exacta wagering. To me, those stats indicate a horse I should consider including in my bets.

CHAPTER 9

FINALIZING THE CHOICES

Now that I have evaluated each entry in the race, I need to narrow it down to the top four horses to consider in my exacta wagers. For this race, and for the sake of money management, I will be investing $34. With that in mind, the goal is to figure out the best way to maximize my bets. Here is how I determined what horses to bet on.

What I will look at each in each race are the 12 pieces of information (my 'dirty dozen') to help me pick my exacta wagers. Some horses might jump out and stand head and shoulders above the others, but the angles might be harder to figure out. Remember that these are only indicators that may help you choose the best horses. Like humans, the ponies don't always perform up to their best ability on a given day. They might not like the surfaces and conditions on race day or just not feel up to their peak performance level. But as long as you are consistent and make wagers based on analyzing the stats, you will have a much better chance to win your bets and maximize your profits.

1. The type of race
2. Surface and condition of the track
3. Length of the race
4. Trainer Stats
5. Jockey Stats
6. The style of horses racing (speed, stalker, closer)
7. A horse's money winnings
8. Statistics about a horse's workouts
9. Ages of the horses racing
10. Tomlinson performance rating
11. Distance performance figures
12. Beyer Speed Figure

Even though I look at these 12 items, I also focus on class, pace and how they race or what I like to call the 'ultimate trip.' There are factors that I weigh more than others. In Chapter 5, I outlined 10 things to help me in my choices. Let's take another look at them:

- The class of races in which the horse has competed
- The style in which a horse races (i.e., a front-runner, a stalker or a closer)
- Time fractions of the races
- The horse's Beyer Speed Figures
- The jockey in each race and the weight carried
- The numbers after the odds (99-10), which is the Standard Speed Rating
- Comments after each race finish
- Works (workout times)
- Trainer stats and information

There are a number of considerations in this list which also are shared by the 'dirty dozen' list. The difference here is to point out that there are some additional stats of which you should be aware when finalizing your choices.

One of the most important things I look at is the Beyer Speed Figure. It is a real indication of how horses race. The higher the number, the better it is. The second thing I look at is how the horse has performed at that distance and type of race. Some horses perform better on shorter distances while others do better at longer ones. Much of that comes from their dam and sire bloodlines. How a horse performs on the type of surface plays a key factor in whether I will include him or her in a wager. The third thing is the class of their entries, looking at whether a horse is moving up or down and how the horse has performed against others. Those, to me, are the top three things I look at.

Some people have asked me about times and how fast horses raced. Certain surfaces and tracks are faster than others. So when it comes down to the top horses, I will then, and only then, look at their final times. Often, you will look at a race and see that one horse has much faster times than another. As long as the horses race at the same track, you can use that as a measure. Obviously, if you have a horse that runs 1:42

Smarter Bets – The Exacta Way

in a particular race and you have another that runs 1:46 in a similar race, you will bet on the faster horse. Times are very important when you are looking at your choices. I usually evaluate the race in-depth before I expend energy comparing the times. If you are a novice, it may be difficult to look at times and compare them at different tracks. If you have been in the racing game for some time, you may have already figured this out. So use them in the sense of a tie-breaker when you are comparing your top choices.

The most difficult part of handicapping this race is when there is no horse that jumps out to me as a front-runner. 'Clement Rock' shows me that he likes to stay close to the front with his running style. But he also has shown he can come from behind, as good closers do. 'Dark Cove,' like 'Clement Rock,' stays close in his racing style, while 'Political Courage' is a closer who loves to come running late in the race. But there is no one horse that stands out to me to as the one that must take the lead. Many times it is much clearer as to how a race will be run. But in this race, it's a tougher call.

My top choice for this race is number 8, 'Dark Cove.' (Figure 25)

Figure 25

Looking at his Beyer Speed Figure of 91 at this distance on the turf, it stands out to me ahead of others in this race. Along with that speed figure, his top turf figure of 95 is higher than all the others. 'Dark Cove' has raced 10 times on turf and won three of them, with 1 second and 1 third-place finish, winning a total of $138,842. Although he has only raced one time at this distance, he has class, having come from Kentucky Derby-winning sire 'Madaglia d'Oro.' While competing against Stakes horses in 2011, he was competitive but not a huge winner mainly because he was racing in higher levels of races. Now he is back racing at a level in which he can be more competitive.

Looking at his history at Gulfstream, 'Dark Cove' clearly likes the track. He has raced three times there on turf with only one win, but his speed figure of 90 is second to only 'Nineinthenine' (91). Remember that horses like some track surfaces more than others. 'Dark Cove' has shown me he likes the track at Gulfstream and should be very competitive in this race.

With a better jockey in Joel Rosario, this race is the horse's second after a layoff and the second after being claimed. 'Dark Cove' came off an 8-month layoff with a 85 Beyer Speed Figure, showing he is in good shape and ready to perform at his top level. Remember the stats of the trainer showing this? 2off180 (12 .17 $0.88) and 31-60days (312 .24 $1.73). These are strong stats to support a good competitor. The statistics for trainer Michael Maker show (55 15 6 8 .27) 2012 (737 159 .22). With 27-percent of his horses winning at this meet, along with 52-percent in the money and 22-percent winners last year, it makes sense to choose this horse as my top pick. If I include the jockey/trainer stats showing how well they do together (J/T 2012 -13 GP (14 .36 $2.37) –a 36-percent winning record, it makes me like him even more. And with the ownership of Kenneth and Sarah Ramsey, top owners of turf horses, 'Dark Cove' lands at the top of my list.

My next selection is a little tougher to make. I like two horses in 'Nineinthenine' and 'Clement Rock.' Each has advantages, so I will narrow it down a little more. Let's start with number 4, 'Nineinthenine.' ***(Figure 26)***

4 Nineinthenine
Own: Elena Arocha
4-1 Purple, White Emblem, Red Star, White — $40,000
SAEZ L (294 48 39 37 .16) 2012: (1220 280 .23)

B. g. 7 (Mar)
Sire: Brushing Up (Broad Brush) $1,500
Dam: Strawberry Custard (First and Only)
Br: Elena Arocha (Fla)
Tr: Toledo Humberto(10 1 0 2 .10) 2012:(43 7 .16)

L 119

Life	65	8	10	8	$225,672	91	D.Fst	7	0	0	0	$3,514 71
2013	1	0	0	1	$4,500	86	Wet(368)	13	1	3	2	$33,472 81
							Synth	0	0	0	0	$0 -
2012	16	3	1	2	$84,114	89	Turf(266)	45	7	7	6	$188,686 91
GP Ⓣ	17	1	1	2	$43,452	91	DstⓉ(288)	7	1	0	1	$25,510 88

24Jan13-9GP	fm	1 1/16 Ⓣ	:23.33 :46.56 1:10.02 1:39.96	4↑Hcp 25000s	86	3	5^4	6^9	7^{10}	5^6	$3^{3½}$	Saez L	L120 b	11.20	94-17	RustlerHustler117[2] Screenply120[1½] Ninithnin120[1]	Settled erly, 5wd lane 9
29Dec12-7GP	fm	1⅛ Ⓣ	:47.29 1:11.04 1:35.48 1:47.72	3↑Hcp 25000s	88	6	9^6	$9^{8½}$	$8^{3¾}$	5^2	$3^{1½}$	Saez L	L120 b	15.00	86-24	Brother Pat117[1] Screenplay119[½] Nineinthenine120[¾]	3wd bid, steady gain 10
8Dec12-6GP	fm	1 1/16 Ⓣ	:24.63 :48.32 1:12.10 1:42.33	3↑Clm 50000	87	2	$6^{6½}$	5^6	$3^{2½}$	$3^½$	4^1	Saez L	L119 b	10.90	85-26	Silver Rock119[nk] Timeless Fashion119[nk] Picou119[½]	Inside bid, willingly 8
10Nov12-11Crc	fm	1⅛ Ⓣ	:49.78 1:14.22 1:38.07 1:49.95	3↑ⓈBHeathTfCH125k	82	4	2^1	$2^½$	2^1	$6^{4½}$	$6^{2¾}$	Saez L	L115 b	6.50	82-17	Bad Debt118[nk] Speak EasyGal112[no] AlleyOopOop116[nk]	Pressed, little left 8
29Sep12-11Crc	fm	7½f Ⓣ	:24.31 :48.08 1:12.51 1:31.19	3↑Alw 25000s	89	4	3	$5^{3¼}$	$5^{1¾}$	$4^{1½}$	$1^{1½}$	Saez L	L120 b	7.50	83-15	Nineinthenine120[1½] BrotherPt118[hd] Riversrunrylee123[2¾]	Edged away late 10
10Aug12-9Crc	yl	1⅛ Ⓣ	:49.98 1:14.55 1:39.94 1:52.10	3↑OC 25k/N2x-N	83	1	5^5	$6^{4½}$	$6^{3¾}$	$2^{1½}$	1no	Silvera R	L123 b	*2.20	74-26	*Nineinthenine*123[no] DinhmiteSl123[5½] NvyWings120[¾]	Saved ground, just up 6
20Jly12-10Crc	gd	1 1/16 Ⓣ	:24.37 :49.31 1:12.82 1:43.42	3↑OC 25k/N2x-N	81	9	$8^{6¼}$	8^6	$8^{3¾}$	$8^{3¼}$	3^{hd}	Silvera R	L123 b	6.30	81-23	DinhmiteSl120[hd] TellTleFriend120[no] *Nineinthnin*123[¾]	Angled wide, missed 9
8Jly12-8Crc	fm	1 1/16 Ⓣ	:24.69 :49.91 1:13.22 1:42.45	3↑Alw 25000s	78	6	$5^{2½}$	4^2	$5^{2¼}$	3^1	1^1	Silvera R	L120 b	6.40	86-13	Nineinthenine120[1] BingoBngoBongo120[2] LibrtyCp120[1½]	Edged away late 7
30Jun12-9Crc	fm	1⅛ Ⓣ	:50.85 1:14.73 1:38.56 1:50.58	3↑OC 25k/N2x-N	76	5	10^5	$11^{5¼}$	$8^{4¼}$	5^8	$4^{5½}$	Rivera J A II	L120 b	10.50	76-23	DevonRock123[5¼] *DinahmiteSal*120[nk] TellTleFriend120[no]	Finished willingly 12
7Jun12-8Crc	yl	1 Ⓣ	:23.83 :48.92 1:12.99 1:36.42	3↑OC 25k/N2x-N	79	5	$5^{4½}$	7^4	$6^{3¼}$	$5^{4¼}$	$4^{3¼}$	Gallardo A A	L120 b	7.50	80-22	*TaleofChmpion*120[1½] *DevonRock*118[1] DinhmiteSl120[¾]	4 wide, mild response 8

WORKS: 20Oct12 Crc 3f fst :37[2] B *14/34* ●24Sep12 Crc 3f wf :37 B *1/10* ●11Feb12 Crc 3f sly :36[2] Bg *1/13* 25May11 Crc 3f fst :39[3] B *11/11* 2Mar11 Crc 3f fst :38[2] B *16/25* 27Jun09 Crc 3f fst :36[4] Bg *9/57*

TRAINER: Turf(20 .15 $1.91) Routes(29 .14 $1.44) Claim(21 .14 $3.35) J/T 2012-13 GP(6 .17 $1.70) J/T 2012-13(8 .25 $3.40)

He looks like one of the more legitimate options to consider in here but don't care to see that the Gulfstream Park turf course hasn't been all that kind to him as he shows just a single win from 17 starts over this turf course; regardless, he commands respect as a contender.

Figure 26

Looking at Beyer Speed Figures, the horse has been very consistent, with 86, 88 and 87 for his last three races at Gulfstream. He has raced seven times at this distance on turf, with his best speed figure being 88. Looking at his figures at Gulfstream on turf, he has raced 17 times with 1 win, 1 second and 2 thirds and a speed figure of 91. That means he likes Gulfstream but probably hasn't been entered in the right race to be competitive. He looks like he is racing from behind the pack, closing in each of his last three races. But the best thing I like about this horse is that it looks like he is improving in speed. On December 8th, he had a time of 1:42.5. I see this by looking at the times of the race and adding 1/5 of a second for every length the horse finishes behind the winner. In his case, he was one length behind, so I added 1/5 of a second to the winning time of 1:42.33 as my handicapper's calculation of how fast he ran. Two races later, on January 24th, he ran the same distance on turf in 1:40-3/5 seconds, which is about 2-seconds faster. 'Nineinthenine' is improving and looks to be a contender.

Looking at workout times, it doesn't appear that this horse has worked out since October 20th. But that doesn't always translate into a win. It seems as if 'Nineinthenine' is doing just fine in three races at Gulfstream of late and showing steady improvement.

Let's take a look at the comments after each race. In his last race, he 'went 5 wide' on the final turn, meaning he had to run all the way around four other horses to have a chance to win. The race before that shows a 3-wide bid and a steady gain. Then, in his first race at Gulfstream since coming over from Calder, it states 'inside bid, willingly,' meaning that jockey Luis Saez positioned him on the inside rail in the home stretch. All of these races were strong closing efforts. The comments seem to be a fair assessment. He hasn't been that competitive at Gulfstream, with only one win in 17 starts, but looks to be a contender at this level. Coming off the more restrictive and more competitive $25,000 Handicap to run this $40,000 Claimer may help his chances here. You can see, three races ago, he was 'in for a tag' (or, could be claimed) of $50,000 and finished only 1 length behind the winner. He seems to be a very consistent horse right now and could be on top if he races his best. I like what I see with this horse showing improvement and good speed figures at this track and I will include him in my exacta wagers.

'Clement Rock' *(Figure 27)* comes into the race with three turf races at this distance and a Beyer Speed Figure of 85. That ranks right up there with the top competitors in this race. In that race where he ran an 85, his share of the purse was a whopping $95,660, which is a large amount, compared to others in this race. As you can see, 'Nineinthenine' also ran his most recent previous race with 'Clement Rock' and finished third. One very important thing I am considering is that if he races like he did last time, closing from behind, he likely will finish in the money. I am not totally convinced he will be second, but he will be in the money. His turf record shows a 50-percent win percentage, which is 5 wins in 10 races. Again, he fits well here.

5 Clement Rock B. h. 5 (Mar)
3-1 Own: Melnyk Racing Stables Inc — Royal Blue, Gold Chevrons, Royal Blue — $40,000
Sire: Strong Hope (Grand Slam) $5,000
Dam: Ellesmere (Tabasco Cat)
Br: Eugene Melnyk (Fla)
Tr: Casse Mark(61 9 10 4 .15) 2012:(675 129 .19)
LEZCANO J (198 43 34 24 .22) 2012: (1052 190 .18) — L 119

Life	11	5	0	0	$249,909	90	D.Fst	0	0	0	0	$0	-
2012	4	1	0	0	$22,905	88	Wet(357)	1	0	0	0	$0	20
2011	7	4	0	0	$227,004	90	Synth	0	0	0	0	$0	-
							Turf(296)	10	5	0	0	$249,909	90
GPⓣ	3	1	0	0	$21,000	88	Dstⓣ(359)	3	1	0	0	$95,660	85

29Dec12-7GP fm 1⅛ ⓣ :47.29 1:11.04 1:35.48 1:47.72 3↑Hcp 25000s 85 8 108½ 1010 95¾ 73½ 52½ Lezcano J L120 b 3.10 85-24 Brother Pat1171 Screenplay119½ Nineinthenine120¾ 5wd, no final kick 10
5Dec12-6GP fm 7½f ⓣ :25.13 :49.75 1:13.61 1:31.22 3↑Clm 25000(25-20) 88 4 7 75½ 65 62 11 Lezcano J L119 b 2.30 78-24 ClementRock1191 TrgetSightd119¾ ConcrtStg119nk Took up start, 5 wide 7
26Aug12-8WO fm 7f ⓣ :23.33 :46.21 1:09.31 1:21.62 3↑PlayKing-G2 86 4 9 85 85 96 76½ Moreno O L117 b 21.00 82-11 BigBandSound1192½ RidingtheRiver123½ *Delegtion*1151½ Off slw,no threat 9
6Aug12-8WO fm 6½f ⓣ :22.79 :45.11 1:08.75 1:15.11 3↑Alw 86820NC 86 3 6 68 66½ 66 62¼ Contreras L L117 b 10.50 89-12 ArticFern118nk Bigstormbrwin119hd StormyRush118nk Willingly but late 6
Previously trained by Pletcher Todd A 2011(as of 12/22): (1000 250 148 159 0.25)
22Dec11-7GP fm 1 ⓣ :24.13 :47.90 1:10.76 1:34.67 3↑OC 100k/c-N 85 5 2½ 2½ 21 32½ 74¼ Castellano J J L120 b 3.80 80-18 *Little Mike*119no Yankee Fourtune1192½ Allie's Event119¾ 3 wide, tired 8
28Oct11-7Bel sf 1 ⓣ :25.28 :50.14 1:14.71 1:39.62 ShdyChrctr60k 90 5 21 21½ 2½ 1hd 1no Castellano J J L122 b 2.70 65-35 ClementRock122no Dynfortwo1182½ TopSurpriz1227¼ 3w, dug in, resolute 6
4Sep11-9Sar fm 1⅛ 🅃 :49.89 1:14.27 1:37.16 1:48.73 Saranac-G3 75 3 84 64½ 74½ 85 96¾ Castro E L123 b 8.40 83-11 BrillintSpeed1172½ Queenspltkittn118½ KingCongi119hd 3w far turn, tired 10
Previously trained by Casse Mark 2011(as of 7/16): (319 68 37 43 0.21)
16Jly11-8WO fm *1⅛ ⓣ :48.66 1:46.98 TorontoCup156k 84 8 21 33 33½ 12 1nk Contreras L L119 b *.70 91-11 ClemntRock119nk ClticConviction119hd RivrLmon116hd Clr str,held drvg 8
25Jun11-4WO gd 1 ⓣ :24.26 :48.27 1:13.00 1:36.59 CBarley100k 88 7 64½ 53½ 53 1hd 12¼ Contreras L L117 b 3.25 78-20 *ClmntRock*1172¼ SmthngExtr117nk ThndrngWtrs1171¾ Blocked,ridden out 8
10Jun11-7WO fm 1$\frac{1}{16}$ ⓣ :23.82 :47.49 1:11.44 1:40.62 3↑Md Sp Wt 61k 83 3 88½ 87¾ 85 23 1½ Contreras L L117 b 11.35 91-16 *ClemntRock*117½ StunningSplit1173¾ DncinDvid123½ Bmp'd,rallied,up late 11
WORKS: 29Jan13 PmMⓣ 5f fm 1:031 B(d) *6/14* 21Jan13 PmMⓣ 5f fm 1:013 B(d) *5/24* 21Dec12 PmMⓣ 5f fm 1:032 B(d) *12/21* 28Nov12 PmMⓣ 5f fm 1:05 B *7/7* 17Nov12 CD 5f fst 1:022 B *24/51* 22Oct12 WO ◈ 5f fst 1:004 B *2/13*
TRAINER: 31-60Days(247 .16 $1.16) Turf(252 .14 $1.17) Routes(427 .18 $1.41) Claim(127 .19 $1.58) J/T 2012-13 GP(13 .46 $4.02) J/T 2012-13(15 .47 $3.72)
Multiple stakes winner chased today's rival Nineinthenine in his latest start, but he's clearly capable of stepping up with a performance that is good enough to get the job done in this spot, and have to respect the fact that he's won five of 10 over turf; Lezcano has won with 4 of 6 (66%) mounts for this barn at the current stand.

Figure 27

As I mentioned previously, a horse comes back from a layoff tends to need a race or two to get back into top shape. With this being his third race off the 3½ month layoff, the distance fits his range. With the exception of the 7½ furlong race, which was his first back from a layoff, his best distance is a range from 1 mile to 1-1/8 miles. 'Clement Rock' has run at higher-level races. If he's ready, he's a player here and likely will be in the money.

Let's now look at the jockey/trainer stats. "J/T 2012-13 GP (13 .46 $4.02) and J/T 2012-13(15 .47 $3.72)"

In 2012 at Gulfstream Park, the jockey-trainer combination of Lezcano and Mark Casse has 46-percent wins out of 13 races, with an average payoff of $4.02. But the best part of that is that Lezcano rode all 13 of his mounts at Gulfstream. Now combine that with the stats for all of 2012, which included two more races (15 total), they won 47-percent of the races. I think that's outstanding and it's a real 'plus' for me.

Let's take a look at the comments at the bottom of the entry. Note that Lezcano has won 4 of 6 (66-percent) of his mounts for his current barn at this meet. The horse has won 5 of his 10 turf starts, winning $249,909, an impressive stat!

'Clement Rock' has worked out twice since his last race. A 5-furlong workout on a firm (fm) turf course on January 29th in 1:03-1/5 was sixth-best out of 14 horses that worked out at that distance that day. His prior workout was on January 21st, in

1:01-3/5 for the same distance. That workout was fifth-best out of 24 at that distance that day.

The thing that concerns me is that he finished fifth in his last race, two places back of 'Nineinthenine,' who is my other choice. Even though he was 10th and closed to finish 5th, the comments show that he was five wide (5wd) and had no final kick. That was his second race off the 3-1/2 month layoff, but it seems he needs to develop a better kick to beat 'Nineinthenine.'

3 Political Courage
Own: Ramona S Bass
6-1 Pink, Yellow Hoops And Bars On Sleeves **$40,000**
ROCCO J S JR (246 32 25 26 .13) 2012: (888 131 .15)

B. g. 4 (Mar)
Sire: Elusive Quality (Gone West) $50,000
Dam: Ladina (Wild Again)
Br: Ramona S Bass (Ky)
Tr: Matz Michael R(51 10 2 4 .20) 2012:(270 34 .13)

L 119

Life	12	3	1	2	$57,675	80
2013	1	1	0	0	$14,700	80
2012	7	2	1	2	$37,328	76
GP Ⓣ	3	2	0	1	$31,605	80

D.Fst	0	0	0	0	$0	-
Wet(384)	3	0	0	1	$8,655	66
Synth	1	0	0	0	$143	57
Turf(319)	8	3	1	1	$48,877	80
DstⓉ(351)	0	0	0	0	$0	-

20Jan13-41GP	fm	1 1/16	Ⓣ	:23.06	:46.52	1:11.86	1:43.79	4↑ Clm 30000(30-25)N3L	80	11	10^{15}	9^{19}	$6^{5\frac{1}{2}}$	$1^{1\frac{1}{2}}$	1^{1}	Rocco J S Jr	L121	7.10	79-28	PoliticlCourge121¹ RivrLmon117hd FoolishTigr121²	Unhurried erly, clear	12
20Dec12-8GP	fm	1 1/16	Ⓣ	:24.77	:49.64	1:14.23	1:44.39	3↑ Clm 30000(30-25)N3L	75	3	10^{11}	$8^{9\frac{1}{2}}$	7^{4}	$4^{2\frac{1}{2}}$	$3^{\frac{3}{4}}$	Rocco J S Jr	L120	8.30	75-24	DynmicBoy118no LoveofFlying121¾ *PoliticlCourge*120nk	Bid btw, late gain	11
7Dec12-6GP	fm	1	Ⓣ	:23.81	:49.21	1:14.28	1:38.79	3↑ Clm 30000(30-25)N2L	70	9	$10^{8\frac{1}{2}}$	$9^{3\frac{1}{2}}$	$8^{3\frac{1}{2}}$	4^{1}	$1^{\frac{3}{4}}$	Rocco J S Jr	L118	6.40	64-28	PoltclCourg118¾ Tzwondrfllf109nk *HoldnBllts*118 1¼	4wide stretch, driving	12
20Oct12-3Del	wf	1 1/16	⊗	:24.59	:49.63	1:14.73	1:47.17	3↑ Clm 25000(25-20)N2L	59	5	5^{4}	$5^{2\frac{1}{2}}$	$4^{\frac{3}{4}}$	3^{2}	3^{5}	Cintron A	L118	*1.10	72-15	FnnyAccomdtn115no PrsdntlClrs124⁵ *PltclCrg*118 1¼	Hung wide, weakened	5
24Sep12-8Del	fm	170	Ⓣ	:23.00	:46.80	1:11.85	1:42.61	3↑ Clm 25000(25-20)N2L	76	1	$7^{5\frac{1}{2}}$	$7^{5\frac{3}{4}}$	7^{5}	$4^{5\frac{1}{2}}$	2^{hd}	Rocco J S Jr	L118	*1.70	81-20	Evensup118hd PoliticalCourage118² DaddyLikesTht118 3¾	Traffic, too late	9
22Aug12-6Sar	fm	1 1/16	Ⓣ	:23.78	:48.48	1:12.30	1:41.37	3↑ Clm 35000B	59	8	9^{10}	10^{10}	9^{10}	10^{12}	$9^{12\frac{1}{2}}$	Bridgmohan S X	L119 b	11.70	83-07	*MsterAchievmnt*117 5¼ *KittnsKid*117½ KnockRock119²	3w 2nd,5w 1/4,outrun	10
27Jly12-5Sar	sly⁵	1 1/8	⊗	:47.66	1:12.52	1:39.21	1:52.63	3↑ OC50k/SAL50k-N	66	5	8^{14}	8^{15}	8^{13}	7^{6}	5^{10}	Rosario J	L117 f	27.75	66-21	CitizenWells117 2½ Bluembr121hd MjsticHop121 6¼	Movd out 1/8,no threat	9
2Jly12-5Del	fm	170	Ⓣ	:22.58	:46.41	1:11.70	1:41.29	3↑ Md 30000(30-25)	73	8	$7^{8\frac{1}{2}}$	6^{7}	$5^{2\frac{1}{2}}$	3^{nk}	$1^{\frac{3}{4}}$	Rocco J S Jr	L120 f	*1.20	88-13	Political Courage120¾ *Airdrop*118⁵ Mikey Joe118½	In traffic, up late	8
30Oct11-7CD	fm	1 1/16	Ⓣ	:24.56	:49.28	1:13.72	1:44.49	Md Sp Wt 42k	72	3	$10^{9\frac{1}{2}}$	10^{14}	$10^{9\frac{1}{4}}$	$5^{5\frac{1}{2}}$	4^{2}	Gomez G K	L118	8.40	75-20	Starforce118¾ Seve118½ Godard118¾	Fought restraint, 5 w	10
7Oct11-6Kee	fst	7f	◈	:22.75	:45.36	1:10.07	1:22.92	Md Sp Wt 49k	57	10	3	2^{1}	2^{1}	6^{6}	7^{11}	Prado E S	L118	28.50	79-08	SvnLivlySins118 1¾ Doctorious118 1¼ GoldnTickt118 1¾	Chased 3 w, faltered	12

WORKS: 2Feb13 PmM 4f fst :50 B *50/75* 13Jan13 PmM 4f fst :47³ B *4/46* 17Dec12 PmM 3f fst :37 B *3/17* 1Dec12 PmM 5f fst 1:02 B *8/9* 24Nov12 PmM 4f fst :48² B *9/18* ● 18Nov12 PmM 3f fst :35³ B *1/4*

TRAINER: WonLastStart(38 .16 $1.87) Turf(172 .15 $2.06) Routes(244 .15 $1.83) Claim(24 .21 $2.32) J/T 2012-13 GP(57 .18 $2.50) J/T 2012-13(125 .18 $1.99)

Certainly respect the way that this stone-cold closer has fired from off the pace in his recent turf attempts, but he's going to need to show up with a career best effort to get the better of these, and it doesn't look like the early pace is going to heat up all that much.

Figure 27

The fourth horse I'm considering is number 3 ***(Figure 27)***, 'Political Courage.' Although I am not totally convinced he should be in my exacta wagers, let's take a look at him anyway. One positive aspect I notice right away is that he has raced three times at Gulfstream, winning two and coming in third once. A downside is that his best speed figure at Gulfstream is only 80. That doesn't compare to the other three horses I previously analyzed, above. The last three races for 'Political Courage' at Gulfstream have been at a lower claiming price of $30,000 and non-winners of 2 or 3 races. Along with that, his speed figures have been 80, 75 and 70, which are much lower than others in this race. With that in mind, I am not sure this horse will be in my top three, let alone my exacta wagers.

I like the way he closed in his last three races. And his turf record is 3 wins, 1 second and 1 third, out of 8 races. That comes to 62-percent in the money. However, he's only won $48,877 in five races on turf, with his best Beyer Speed Figure being 80. With all this information, I am not convinced he will be a strong contender. I think going to a $40,000 Claiming race, which is stepping up from his past three races, may be just a little too difficult for him. He may need a few more races at this level, but I think he may be a better fit at lower levels. Therefore, I will remove him from consideration and will 'pass' on including him in my exacta wagers.

CHAPTER 10

WANNA BET?

As a true handicapper, you must always set your financial limits for each race. Consider the dollar amount you potentially could lose before deciding on a bet.

With that in mind, my bet for this race will be a total of $34. But the difficulty here is that no one horse stands out to be significantly better than the others. I will bet two types of exacta wagers, with a goal of maximizing my winnings.

Let's take a good look at it. The first bet I made was an exacta wheel. My top choice here was #8, 'Dark Cove.' My second and third choices were #4, 'Nineinthenine,' and #5, 'Clement Rock.' I went to the window and asked for a $5 exacta, with the #8 to win, over the #4 and #5. This actually is two separate $5 bets: the 8 over the 4 and the 8 over the 5, for a total outlay of $10.

My second wager was an exacta box with the same three horses. I liked the same horses as above, the 8, 4 and 5, except they are boxed together. This is a total of six exacta wagers: the 8/4, 4/8, 4/5, 5/4, 8/5, 5/8. I went to the window and asked for a $4 exacta box with 8, 4 and 5. The total cost of this wager was $24. I bet it this way because if I was correct with the horses but not correct with the order of finish, I still would collect on my bet. If I was correct in my first bet (the exacta wheel), I also would collect on the exacta box.

You have to be 'smarter' with your bets. Remember that the idea in exacta wagering is to consider all the handicapping factors and make a wise choice to profit from your picks. Not every race runs true to form, but if you use concepts like my 'dirty dozen' and a prudent thought process to make your choices, you will have a much higher winning percentage and maximize your profits. With that in mind, let's now review the results of this race.

FIFTH RACE
Gulfstream
FEBRUARY 10, 2013

1⅛ MILES. (Turf) (1.44^{2}) CLAIMING. Purse $42,500 (includes $8,500 FOA – Florida Owners Awards) FOR FOUR YEAR OLDS AND UPWARD. Weight, 123 lbs. Non–winners of a race at a mile or over since January 10 Allowed 2 lbs. Such a race since December 10, 2012 Allowed 4 lbs. Claiming Price $40,000 (Races Where Entered For $30,000 Or Less Not Considered) (Condition Eligibility). (If deemed inadvisable to run this race over the turf course, it will be run on the main track at One Mile and One Eighth) (Rail at 48 feet).

Value of Race: $36,550 Winner $20,400; second $8,840; third $4,250; fourth $1,700; fifth $340; sixth $340; seventh $340; eighth $340. Mutuel Pool $279,471.00 Exacta Pool $223,594.00 Trifecta Pool $144,232.00 Superfecta Pool $93,999.00

Last Raced	Horse	M/Eqt.	A.	Wt	PP	St	¼	½	¾	Str	Fin	Jockey	Cl'g Pr	Odds $1
5Jan13 ^{7}FG^{4}	Dark Cove	L	6	119	8	3	$2^{1\frac{1}{2}}$	$2^{1\frac{1}{2}}$	3^{3}	$2^{2\frac{1}{2}}$	$1^{\frac{3}{4}}$	Rosario J	40000	*2.30
24Jan13 ^{9}GP^{3}	Nineinthenine	L b	7	119	4	1	5^{2}	$5^{2\frac{1}{2}}$	4^{1}	$3^{\frac{1}{2}}$	2^{nk}	Saez L	40000	4.90
29Dec12 ^{7}GP^{5}	Clement Rock	L b	5	119	5	6	$3^{1\frac{1}{2}}$	3^{2}	2^{hd}	$1^{\frac{1}{2}}$	3^{nk}	Lezcano J	40000	2.30
20Jan13 ^{11}GP^{1}	Political Courage	L	4	119	3	5	6^{3}	$6^{1\frac{1}{2}}$	6^{3}	4^{2}	$4^{5\frac{3}{4}}$	Rocco J S Jr	40000	6.10
28Dec12 ^{3}GP^{9}	Julius Geezer-Ire	L	5	119	1	2	1^{1}	$1^{1\frac{1}{2}}$	1^{hd}	5^{5}	$5^{\frac{3}{4}}$	Lanerie C J	40000	29.30
12Jan13 ^{8}GP^{7}	Minnie Punt	L b	7	119	7	8	7^{hd}	7^{hd}	8	6^{2}	$6^{4\frac{1}{4}}$	Castellano J J	40000	3.80
2Feb13 ^{7}GP^{10}	Decaf Again	L bf	7	119	6	7	8	8	7^{hd}	8	$7^{\frac{1}{2}}$	Delgado J N	40000	75.80
19Jan13 ^{2}GP^{6}	Ojibway Signal	L b	5	119	2	4	4^{1}	4^{hd}	$5^{1\frac{1}{2}}$	$7^{1\frac{1}{2}}$	8	Contreras L	40000	19.10

***–Actual Betting Favorite.**

OFF AT 2:39 Start Good. Won driving. Course firm.

TIME :23^{3}, :47^{4}, 1:11^{2}, 1:34^{3}, 1:46^{4} (:23.60, :47.81, 1:11.50, 1:34.62, 1:46.98)

$2 Mutuel Prices:				
	8 –DARK COVE	6.60	3.80	2.60
	4 –NINEINTHENINE		4.60	2.80
	5 –CLEMENT ROCK			2.60

$2 EXACTA 8–4 PAID $29.00 $1 TRIFECTA 8–4–5 PAID $29.40
$1 SUPERFECTA 8–4–5–3 PAID $108.60

B. h, (Apr), by Medaglia d'Oro – Crystal Cove, by Kris S.. Trainer Maker Michael J. Bred by Stonewall Farm Stallions (Ky).

DARK COVE stalked the pace, rallied to reach even terms for command with CLEMENT ROCK on the far turn, then dueled with that rival to deep stretch and prevailed. NINEINTHENINE rated off the pace, eased out for the stretch run and rallied to be up for the place. CLEMENT ROCK tracked the pace, rallied three wide to reach even terms for command on the far turn, then dueled with DARK COVE to deep stretch and weakened. POLITICAL COURAGE reserved racing along the inside, angled out leaving the far turn and finished willingly to just miss the show. JULIUS GEEZER (IRE) set the pace along the rail into the far turn and tired. MINNIE PUNT was not a factor. DECAF AGAIN was outrun. OJIBWAY SIGNAL tracked the leaders three wide into the far turn, then faltered.

Owners– 1, Ramsey Kenneth L and Sarah K; 2, Arocha Elena; 3, Melnyk Racing Stables Inc; 4, Bass Ramona S; 5, Wildcard Racing Syndicate; 6, Marjac Pino Stable and Bommarito Vincent; 7, Rose Family Stable; 8, Bell David R and Vlahos Gus

Trainers– 1, Maker Michael J; 2, Toledo Humberto; 3, Casse Mark; 4, Matz Michael R; 5, Weaver Amy; 6, Braddy J David; 7, Rose Barry R; 8, Bell David R

Nineinthenine was claimed by Treblanna Stable; trainer, Volk Scott.

$2 Daily Double (3–8) Paid $10.60 ; Daily Double Pool $43,804 .
$1 Pick Three (9–3–8) Paid $20.90 ; Pick Three Pool $65,995 .
$1 Pick Four (6–9–3–8) Paid $152.40 ; Pick Four Pool $143,418 .

Copyright © 2013 Daily Racing Form, Inc. and Equibase Company, all rights reserved

Data provided or compiled by Daily Racing Form, Inc. and Equibase Company generally are accurate but occasionally errors and omissions occur as a result of incorrect data received from others, mistakes in processing and other causes. Daily Racing Form, Inc. and Equibase Company disclaim responsibility for the consequences, if any, of such errors, but would appreciate their being called to their attention.

Figure 28

As you can see from the results *(Figure 28)*, my bets paid off. 'Dark Cove,' #8, won the race, with #4, 'Nineinthenine,' coming in second. The $2 exacta paid $29. Here's the breakdown:

My first winning bet was a $5 exacta box wager (costing $10) of 8/4 that returned $72.50, so that was a profit of $62.50. My second winning bet was a $4 exacta box (costing $24 total) 8/4/5. The winning portion, 8/4, paid me $58. My profit was $34.

I'd put up $34, won $130.50 and gained a net profit of $96.50. Making smarter bets, the exacta way, really paid off! The winner, 'Dark Cove,' went off as the 2-1 favorite and beat 'Nineinthenine' by three-quarters of a length. 'Nineinthenine' went off at about 5-1, was the fourth betting favorite and beat 'Clement Rock' by only a neck. Looking back at my picks, they ran true to form and finished just as I handicapped them. Remember, we're trying to find the winner and the right horses to include in your exacta wagers. 'Clement Rock' looked good and was in the money, finishing in third by only a neck. 'Dark Cove' stalked the pace, staying close to the front but not pressing too hard. Joel Rosario rode a perfect race, finishing three-quarters of a length ahead of the next two horses. There was one claim, 'Nineinthenine,' who got picked up for the $40,000 claiming price by Treblenna Stables and trainer Scott Volk.

The results chart displays a lot of information you may be able to use for future races. The first thing that I look at is 'Last Raced,' which shows the last time the horse raced and where. In the case of 'Dark Cove,' it was January 3rd at FG, which is Fair Grounds. Granted, that's on the form we used for handicapping the race. But if you obtained this information after the race and didn't have the form to consult, it helps you see where horses come from and the length of time since their last races.

The next thing the results chart shows me is how they raced. 'Dark Cove' is a 6-year-old (6) and carried 119 pounds. He started from the 8th position and broke 3rd at the start. Each time fraction, the ¼ mile pole, ½ mile pole, ¾ mile pole, the stretch and then the finish, shows where this horse was at that point of the race. In this case, 'Dark Cove' stayed up close, racing 2nd and then winning by ¾ of a length. The jockey was Rosario and the claiming price was $40,000, same as the rest of the field. The final winning payout was at odds of $2.30 for a $1 bet, paying $6.60 to win. Remember, that means you win $2.30 for each $1 you bet, plus your original $2 bet back. That is how they came up with $6.60 for the win bet.

Smarter Bets – The Exacta Way

Other tidbits of information you can glean are who owned the horses and who trained them. And as you can see from the comments under the trainer's information, 'Nineinthenine' was claimed by Treblanna Stables and their new trainer, Scott Volk. Additionally, you can see payouts for each type of bet, the fractions set by the lead horse, breeding information, and race specifics like distance, type of surface, the purse and the conditions for that race. Lastly, you can see each horse's payout based on finish position.

Considering the fractions set by the lead horse, the first ¼-mile was run in 23-3/5 seconds, followed by: 47-4/5, 1:11-2/5, 1:34-3/5 and a finishing time of 1:46-4/5. I previously mentioned that different race tracks may show faster or slower times for similar races. In the case of 'Dark Cove,' his last race at Fair Grounds was run at the same distance of this race but with the time of 1:50-2/5. This race was won with the time of 1:46-4/5, almost four seconds faster. He may appear to have run faster today, but most likely the times at the Fair Grounds are a little slower due to the track surface. That is why winning times should not be used as the only handicapping factor, because times differ from track to track.

When you are deciding to wager on exactas, be sure to take the time and utilize the process I go through to narrow your selections down to your top horses. You may find a great angle that pays larger profits than others. Taking a favorite may not always pay off but, if so, there should be a good reason to make the favorite your top pick.

Every race is different. Don't feel that you must bet each and every one. I know it is fun and you may feel like you have the need to bet every race, but you really don't need to. Remember, you are here to make money. If you are there for entertainment, feel free to take a break and handicap the next race. But take the time to look things over and make notes on your forms. Bring a pen and don't hesitate to markup that form. I spend a lot of time researching my choices with the Daily Racing Form the day before I go to the races. It gives me a lot of time to look things over, and I do so more than once. On occasion I see something special that jumps out at me. But by taking extra time, I feel I can digest and analyze what is most important to me. Then I make my selections.

I also find it helpful to visually look over the horses by visiting the paddock before the race (the public is permitted to do that). A horse may appear to be over-anxious, sweaty, nervous or simply lackadaisical. In my second book, 'Inside the Sport of Kings,' these factors are mentioned in the chapter 'Looks Won't Deceive.' There is nothing worse than picking a horse on paper and finding out he doesn't look good on the track. Remember you are here to learn to make 'Smarter Bets – the Exacta Way.'

CHAPTER 11

THE KENTUCKY DERBY – THEN AND NOW

Known as the 'the fastest two minutes in sports,' the Kentucky Derby has become known as the most prestigious horse race in the world. It has grown to be my favorite race. Held each year on the first Saturday in May, Louisville's Churchill Downs explodes with excitement and crowds that have grown to over 150,000 for the first leg of horse racing's Triple Crown.

Once known as the Louisville Jockey Club, Churchill Downs has been known for many long-standing traditions. One of the most popular surrounds the Mint Julep. It's a cold, iced drink made with crushed ice, the best Kentucky bourbon you can find, white sugar and mint leaves.

According to the International Bartenders Association, a mint julep is made with 2 fluid ounces of Bourbon whiskey, 4 mint leaves, 1 teaspoon powdered sugar and 2 teaspoons water. Preparation consists of 'muddling' (gently crushing) the mint, sugar and water in a highball glass to release essential oils and intensify the flavor. You then fill the glass with cracked ice, add the Bourbon and stir well until the outside of the glass becomes frosted. Garnish with a sprig of mint.

The traditional way to serve a Mint Julep is in a silver or pewter cup. For many who attend the Kentucky Derby, Churchill Downs offers the cocktail in an official keepsake glass etched with a list of all the past winners. Every year, this glass is commissioned and changed to offer race patrons and collectors something by which to remember their visit to the Derby. These collectable glasses were first offered in 1939 and have risen in value over the years. Each year, Derby-goers look forward to the new design and the accompanying minty taste of a Julep.

Another tradition is Burgoo, which is a thick stew of beef, chicken, pork and vegetables. It's a very popular Southern dish that is served at the Kentucky Derby. This one hasn't been high on my Derby Favorites list, but many who have indulged in this tasty dish say it is something to enjoy. With the huge diversity within the crowds, the food varies between different areas of the track. While things have changed recently with regards to what you can and can't bring in to the track, infield spectators and party-goers still have been known to bring their own picnic lunches or try the endless variety of sumptuous nourishment available from the many vendors.

My favorites are the barbeque dishes, smothered with Southern sweet and spicy sauce that drips down the sides of the sweet buns. If you have never attended the Kentucky Derby, you really need to visit the infield for an experience of a lifetime.

The Friday before the Derby (known as 'Oaks Day') features the Kentucky Oaks, a race for three-year-old fillies that is the equivalent to the Kentucky Derby, which is for any three-year-old. Oaks Day attracts a much more manageable crowd that numbers approximately 110,000 attendees, versus the 150,000 – 160,000 race patrons who visit for the Kentucky Derby on Saturday. Among the infield crowd, many more locals visit the track to enjoy the day on Friday, in contrast to Saturday that is filled with many more out-of-towners who primarily are there to party. Both days are interesting, but I have grown to prefer the infield on Friday and enjoy a seat in the grandstand on Saturday.

On both Friday and Saturday, party patrons begin lining up outside the track to await the moment the gates open, which is 8am. Jammed together, visitors make their way into the infield grassy areas to stake their space, set up and prepare for a long day of racing. In previous years, many would pull wagons full of chairs, food, coolers and assorted sundries to make it easier to carry everything. But with the most recent changes at Churchill Downs, coolers, wagons and tents no longer are allowed.

Fans can reach the infield through the tunnel that extends from the east entrance and goes directly underneath the track. A more manageable way to reach the infield is to use the tunnel that runs from the grandstand area and goes below the track.

Smarter Bets – The Exacta Way

In contrast to the party-goers who flood the infield on both Friday and Saturday, there are great number of seats in the grandstands. Many who are lucky enough to obtain these seats have a much different experience, with Millionaires Row offering the most expensive and the more exclusive seats. Fashion is the number one thing you will notice as a highlight of the day. Women traditionally have strutted in wearing beautiful, colorful dresses and large, lavish and extravagant hats, while men are dressed in suits suitable for a traditional Southern Gentleman. Noticeably, you look around and appreciate the fashion statement that stands as a highlight of the day. Everyone wants to get dressed up and look his or her best. It's the Derby!

The front gate to Churchill Downs features a beautiful statue honoring 'Barbaro.' Many of the patrons stop to get their pictures in front of the 2006 Derby winner before passing through the beautiful gated entry.

As you may recall, after winning the '06 Kentucky Derby, 'Barbaro' raced in the second leg of the Triple Crown, the Preakness Stakes. A heavy favorite, the 3-year-old unfortunately fractured bones in his right rear leg during the race, later developed the disease Laminitis in all four legs and was euthanized the following year. The statue commemorates a true Triple Crown contender whose life was tragically cut short.

But whether you are sitting in the grandstands areas or have the more costly seats upstairs, I feel truly in awe every time I enter the historic Churchill Downs.

One of my favorite moments at the Kentucky Derby is the singing of 'My Old Kentucky Home.' This Stephen Foster song is the state song of Kentucky and traditionally is sung while the horses are walked in front of the grandstands prior to the Derby race. This is known as post parade. This long-standing tradition began back in 1924 and to this day is a highlight of the Derby. I always get chills when the University of Louisville's marching band strikes up and the first words are sung. The entire crowd stops what they're doing and everyone sings, whether they know the words or not:

The sun shines bright in My Old Kentucky Home,
'Tis summer, the people are gay;
The corn-top's ripe and the meadow's in the bloom
While the birds make music all the day.
The young folks roll on the little cabin floor,
All merry, all happy and bright;
By 'n' by hard times comes a knocking at the door,
Then My Old Kentucky Home, good night!

(Chorus)

Weep no more my lady
Oh weep no more today;
We will sing one song
For My Old Kentucky Home
For My Old Kentucky Home, far away

Then there is the race itself. Everyone is on their feet as the horses arrive at the gate. Bursting with anticipation, the crowd excitement builds until the bell sounds and the track announcer belts, "--aaaand they're off!" People begin yelling and screaming and you suddenly hear all the names of all the horses, all at once. It's amazing what you hear at that moment.

The horses then thunder down the long first stretch of the mile-and-1/4 race in front of the grandstands, jockeying for position before entering the first turn. They make their way to the backstretch before the final turn and head down the homestretch. It is a powerful and dramatic culmination of the most exciting two minutes in sports as the horses jockey for position and make their final push toward the finish line.

At the conclusion of the Derby race and after the horses return to the grandstand area, the winner has the honor of entering the prestigious Winner's Circle. In front of the 150,000-plus crowd, the winning horse in the Run for the Roses is draped in the traditional garland while the governor of the Commonwealth of Kentucky awards the winner the trophy. What a sight that is, with the owners, their friends, the winning trainer and jockey all joining in on the success!

Smarter Bets – The Exacta Way

Like many, I have incepted my own traditions. I begin planning for the Derby at least eight months prior to the race. It differs each year, and can include a few rounds of golf, bourbon and horse farm tours, the Thunder over Louisville air show (which features the largest annual fireworks display in North America), the Great Balloon Race, the Great Steamboat Race featuring the Belle of Louisville, the Pegasus Parade (one of the largest parades in the United States), the Kentucky Derby Festival Chow Wagon riverfront party and the Derby Marathon and mini-Marathon. All of these events take place in the two weeks leading up to and culminating with the Kentucky Derby.

My first Kentucky Derby was in 1974. As I mentioned earlier, I was a young 18-year-old high school senior who was lucky enough to be invited to the Derby. My friend Greg had asked me to go, and only after receiving approval from my father did I hop into my Ford Galaxy 500 and head south to Louisville. We were going to stay with Greg's friends who lived in a very affluent area of Louisville. This was going to be the 100th running of the Kentucky Derby and a huge milestone. Just one year prior to this in 1973, 'Secretariat' had set a Kentucky Derby record for being the fastest winner in the history of the race and went on to win the Triple Crown.

One year, while we were traveling down to Kentucky, bad weather struck Louisville. A tornado destroyed or damaged many homes, and my friend's parents' house was one of them. When we arrived to see the home, it was barely standing and half gone. It was an unreal site and something I have only seen on television. The area seemed devastated. One house was demolished while the house next door was completely untouched. Not a thing had happened to the neighbor's home while the Campbell's house (where we were intending to stay) was torn to shreds. Windows were blown out, walls were missing from half the house and debris was strewn all over the neighborhood. So, due to the unfortunate tornado damage, we stayed at the University of Louisville Youth Hostel. Called the 'Red Barn' and located in the heart of the campus, this renovated barn had cement floors, a stage at one end and tables at the other. It was simple housing that offered showers to all the people who stayed there. It also was about a 15-minute walk to the track. If I recall correctly, it cost $5 per night to stay there. You staked out a spot and put your sleeping bag and clothes down on the ground. I can remember stepping over people to get to our small area late in the night. And the only way to get in was to have a wristband that showed you paid your fee. They served Krispy Crème donuts in the morning and we were able to walk right across the street to the gym for a shower. With the number of people who used the facilities, it wasn't very pleasant. But it was a great perk for all who didn't mind using them.

On Saturday, May 4th, 1974, we made we made our way through the front gates and crowded turnstiles of Churchill Downs. It was a huge mass of humanity of a bigger proportion than I had ever experienced. There was only one way to get from the clubhouse and grandstands to the infield, and that was through the tunnel under the grandstands. Shoulder to shoulder, we walked at a snail's pace through this huge passageway that entered into the infield. People were yelling and screaming. There was whistling and shouting and we then came to a literal standstill. At one point, I think my feet were picked off the ground and we were so smashed together that I didn't fall. Since then, my perception is that Churchill Downs is more conscious of the safety aspect of a mass of humanity passing through the tunnels.

Once we reached the infield we staked our ground, which was at the final turn of the track and where many of Greg's friends, students from the University of Kentucky, usually went. I remember it being a partially cloudy day with times of sunshine, with temps only in the mid-60s.

The crowd was the biggest I had ever seen, later turning out to be a record 163,628 people. It took forever to make our way to any part of the infield. The bathroom lines were ridiculous, as were those at the betting windows --it's a wonder we ever 'made it.'

The winning horse that year was 'Cannonade,' a sleek, good-looking bay colt who was a favorite. Winning by 2¼ lengths over 'Hudson Country,' this 5-1 shot paid $5 to win, $3 to place and $2.40 to show. I was fortunate enough to have placed a bet (I can't recall how much) on 'Cannonade' – and this was my very first Derby!

'Cannonade' was coupled as one entry with another horse, 'Judger,' an eighth-place finisher ridden by Laffitt Pincay, Jr. 'Cannonade' came out of the 2nd post position and opened slowly. He raced 12th at the ¼ pole, moved up to 11th at the half mile, slipped to 5th by the ¾ pole, was 1st at the mile pole and never looked back, beating 'Hudson Country' by 2¼ lengths. The time he ran was 2:04, which was 5 seconds slower than the record set by 'Secretariat' only one year before and the best of 23

Smarter Bets – The Exacta Way

horses that day. Unfortunately, 'Cannonade' went on to finish 3rd in the next two legs of the Triple Crown, the Preakness Stakes and the Belmont Stakes.

By the way, I met Angel Cordero, Jr. (who rode 'Cannonade' that year) a couple years ago at an autograph signing at a sports collectibles convention. I presented him my race program from 1974 and told him that was the very first Kentucky Derby I ever attended. He signed my program and told me that the '74 race also was the first Derby in which he'd ever ridden –and he won it! As our photograph was snapped, we looked at each other and shared a smile *(Figure 29)*.

Figure 29

One interesting fact I have observed about Kentucky Derby horses is that the winners usually come from behind and close on the rest of the field. Very seldom do horses win this race with a front-running style. The only front-runner I can recall in my time is 'War Emblem,' trained by Bob Baffert, in 2002. He flew from the gate and never looked back. He ran wire-to-wire in fractions of 23.25, 47.04, 1:11.75, 1:36.70 and finishing the race in 2:01.13. 'War Emblem' had come into that race the winner of the Illinois Derby, which seldom saw horses finish well in the Derby. He wasn't one of my picks on that day. My horse was 'Medaglio d'Oro,' who finished 4th. Following my thought process, I never pick a front-runner in the Derby, but what a mistake that was! 'War Emblem' went off at 20-1 and paid $43 to win, $22.80 to place and $13.60 to show. The $2 exacta paid a whopping $1,300.80, with the trifecta paying an unheard-of amount: $18,373.20. This only happened because of the longshots that finished 1-2-3. The second-place horse was 'Proud Citizen,' who went off at 23-1, and third-place finisher 'Perfect Drift,' which was 8-1 at post time. That was the year I knew exactas were going to be a part of my betting vocabulary from then on.

I have attended the Kentucky Derby every year since 1974, with the exception of one. That was 1981, when my son Philip (PJ) was born. Originally, the doctor had given my wife and me an estimated due date of early May for his birth. With this in mind, I was staying close to home as the arrival of our first child was drawing near. But as it turned out, the doctors were way off and PJ was born on May 20, 1981. So instead of attending the Kentucky Derby in person, my entire neighborhood got together to have a Derby party. That year, 3-1 'Pleasant Colony' won the Kentucky Derby over 'Wood Chopper,' a 34-1 longshot. 'Pleasant Colony' went on to win the Preakness and finished 3rd in the Belmont Stakes, just missing the elusive Triple Crown. But the real winner that year was our family, as Philip Justin Hoffman was born.

For years, my annual pilgrimage to Kentucky for the Derby involved another tradition, a Pre-Derby party at the home of Bob and Teri Brabec-Ciskoski. Teri is the sister of my old college roommate, Frank Brabec. After the long day of racing on Friday, we all would head back to the hotel, shower, change clothes and then get together with a group of Derby friends. We ate and drank, played music and discussed who we liked to for the Derby race the next day. Everyone had their opinions, some smarter than others, but we all listened and tried to determine the winner. And in 1995, it turned out that I picked the right horse.

Famed trainer D. Wayne Lucas had entered three horses that year. Two of them were 'Timber Country,' a two-year-old champion male, and 'Serena's Song,' a filly that was the 3.40-1 favorite. Both of these horses were great. But the third horse Lucas trained and entered was eventual winner 'Thunder Gulch,' which came into this race as the winner of the Gulfstream Park Fountain of Youth and the Florida Derby. The question I asked myself was why a D. Wayne Lucas horse would go off at such high odds after winning these two prestigious races? At that time, 'Thunder Gulch' was my choice and I was going to bet on this horse across the board: win, place and show. And boy did that pay off! I had mentioned this horse to the others that night at the party and they all thought I was crazy. 'Timber Country' and 'Serena's Song' were coupled and many savvy handicappers expected them to win. But on this day, I decided to take the other Lucas-trained horse.

I watched, and to my amazement, he ran in the top six for three-fourths of the race and then closed, like all good Derby winners do, to win by 2¼ lengths at 24-1. Needless to say, I won big! 'Serena's Song' was a front-runner. She had taken off from the start and ran 1st for the first mile in a very respectable 1:35, then started to fade. I thought the fractions for the race were fast. The first quarter mile was in 22.57, with fractions of 45.89 for half, 1:10.33 for ¾ miles and the mile in 1:35.72, while the winner, 'Timber Country,' finished in 2:01.27. In contrast, 'Timber Country' started far back, from the 15th position, and ran near the back of the pack for much of the race. When he hit the stretch, he was 10th and began to close, while 'Thunder Gulch' was first at the top of the stretch. When they hit the wire, 8-1 shot 'Tejano Run' was trying to catch the winner and finished only a head in front of the fast-closing 'Timber Country.' 'Thunder Gulch' opened his winning margin and surged to 2¼-length victory, a fantastic finish! Jockey Gary Stevens had won the Derby on a 24-1 longshot, and I had bet on him.

Everyone I'd spoken with at the party was totally in shock after the race. I had picked a winner. And not only a winner, but a 24-1 longshot winner. Some of my Derby friends had listened to my reasoning and included it in their trifectas. While they didn't have the outright winner, they won $12,000 in their trifecta box bets, only because I had suggested they also bet on my horse. That was a very memorable and profitable Kentucky Derby race for all of us.

Over the years, many different friends and college roommates have joined me at the Derby. Some have attended for a few years, and others have been there, then taken time off and come back again for the sheer enjoyment of the party. But for me, having enjoyed the Kentucky Derby experience for 41 of the past 42 years, it's become a melding of enduring friendships, traditions and a plethora of varied, fun activities.

In 2001, I decided to bring my wife and children. My son was 20-years-old and my daughter was 19. While my wife really didn't like the whole Derby experience, we went as a family. We stayed at the Holiday Inn just a few miles from Churchill Downs. I had never stayed in this hotel, but they offered free transportation to the track and back, and that appealed to me. It was my wife's second time and my kids' first and only trip to the Derby with me.

We had eaten breakfast on Saturday in the restaurant, which at that timed was called the Monarch Room. After a hearty meal, we boarded the bus and took a 5-minute ride to Churchill Downs. We didn't have grandstand tickets for Saturday but knew we would be meeting some friends I knew in the infield location where I had been going. We were near the center of the racetrack, just off the walking path and west of the bathrooms and betting windows. We set up our chairs and got ready to soak up the sun. It was a hot, sunny day that hit about 86 degrees but, unfortunately, it didn't turn out to be a very profitable day. My son and my wife really didn't like the crowds. There were too many people partying like fools, they weren't enjoying themselves and the two of them returned to the hotel before the race actually started. That left my daughter, Cristina, and me to the race.

The favorite that year was 'Point Given,' a big horse trained by Bob Baffert and ridden by Gary Stevens. As much as I liked both the trainer and jockey, I just couldn't bet on the favorite. Many favorites don't win the Derby and I didn't really think this was the year it was going to happen. My first choice was 'Millennium Wind.' He was ridden by Laffitt Pincay, Jr., went off at 10-1 and ended up coming in 11th place. I didn't think he was a bad horse, he just happened to run a bad race that day.

'Songandaprayer' broke quickly to the lead and held it for the first 3/4 of a mile. He went off at 35-1 odds and wasn't a factor at all in the race. 'Balto Star' followed along in second and faded badly, along with most of the field. The horse that shocked me was the third-place finisher, 'Congaree.' This 7-1 shot was in first at the top of the stretch but just couldn't hold on. He had overtaken 'Point Given' at the mile marker and was passed by 'Invisible Ink,' a 55-1 longshot who beat him by a nose, and the winner, 'Monarchos,' who won by 4¾ lengths. It was a special day for owner John Oxley. 'Monarchos' had run the second-fastest Kentucky Derby in history, only 2/5 of a second slower than 'Secretariat.' The winning time was 1:59-4/5 seconds. If only I had thought more about this horse, named 'Monarchos,' since I had eaten breakfast a few hours earlier in the 'Monarch Room' of the Holiday Inn! He had won the Florida Derby, which I have always held in high regard. And now he won, paying $23.00/$11.80/$8.80. But that was just part of the story. The exacta paid $1,229 for a simple $2 wager. That was the moment I began thinking I should start betting more exactas. 'Invisible Ink' was a 55-1 longshot for second, paying $46.60 for place and $21.20 for show. Boy, did I miss that one!

I have had my share of winners in the Kentucky Derby: 'Sunday Silence' in 1989 at 3-1, 'Lil E Tee' in 1992 at 16-1, 'Thunder Gulch' in 1995 at 24-1 and 'Silver Charm' in 1997 at 4-1. I bet the favorite, 'Fusaichi Pegasus,' in 2000 at 2-1, 'Street Sense' in 2007 at 4-1 and 'Big Brown' in 2008 at 2-1. But like many Derby gamblers, I have wagered on many horses that have finished 2nd, 3rd or out of the money. It has become a very difficult race to bet because of the huge 20-horse fields, but it is always interesting, to say the least.

When I first attended the 1974 Derby with my good friend Greg, known as 'Doc,' I used to narrow it down to two horses on which to bet. I would then ask Doc what horse he thought we should bet. Many times he would pick the gray horse, way before the time they became popular. For years, many people would place wagers based on trivialities like a horse's color. In the 1970s, gray horses were not popular with breeders or bettors. It was a fact, not just a superstition, that few gray-colored horses won races.

But Doc wasn't the best handicapper. So if he told me to pick one horse, I would pick the other one, most times winning my bet. But on the other hand, everyone has a 'lucky pick' every once in a while.

In 2009, my good friend Jim Provenzale *(Figure 30)* came along with me for his first Derby. The first thing you need to know about Jim is that he isn't a handicapper. But on May 2nd, 2009, Jim was the biggest winner of us all. Sitting on bleacher-style bench seats in the grandstands, picking our horses, I leaned over and asked Jim what horse he had bet. He didn't want to jinx himself, so he didn't tell me. After all the horses had crossed the finish line, he was ecstatic because he had bet on the winner. That horse was number 8, 'Mine That Bird,' which went off at 50-1. He closed on the field and won handily, beating my horse, 'Pioneer of the Nile,' by 6¾ lengths. If I had only known, I could have boxed our horses for a huge payoff. That exacta paid $2,074.80. The best part of the story is when I asked Jim how he picked that horse. He told me it was easy: he was married in August, the 8th month of 1988, so he bet $8 across the board on number 8. For a $24 bet, he collected $732.

Figure 30

Exacta betting in the Kentucky Derby race has always proved to be a great payoff. The first Derby to offer exacta wagering was in 1985. On that day, 'Spend A Buck,' a 4-1 horse, beat longshot 'Stephans Odyssey' (13-1) to pay $118.20 for a $2 bet. Since then, exacta wagering has paid off well for crafty bettors at the Kentucky Derby. Below you will see all the exacta winnings since 1985:

Smarter Bets – The Exacta Way

Year	Winner & Place Horse	$2 Exacta Payout
1985	Spend A Buck (4-1) & Stephans Odyssey (13-1)	$118.20
1986	Ferdinand (17-1) & Bold Arrangement (9-1)	$385.00
1987	Alysheba (8-1) & Bet Twice (10-1) (my choice)	$109.60
1989	Sunday Silence (3-1) & Easy Goer (.80-1)	$15.20
1990	Unbridled (10-1) & Summer Squall (2-1)	$65.80
1991	Strike the Gold (4-1) & Best Pal (5-1) (my choice)	$73.40
1992	Lil E Tee (16-1)(my choice) & Casual Lies (30-1)	$854.40
1993	Sea Hero (13-1) & Prairie Bayou (4-1)(my choice)	$190.60
1994	Go for Gin (9-1) & Strodes Creek (7-1)	$184.80
1995	Thunder Gulch (24-1) (my choice) & Tejano Run (8-1)	$480.00
1996	Grindstone (5-1) (my choice) & Cavonnier (5-1)	$61.80
1997	Silver Charm (4-1) (my choice) & Captain Bodget (3-1)	$31.00
1998	Real Quiet (8-1) & Victory Gallop (14-1) (my choice)	$291.80
1999	Charismatic (31-1) & Menifee (7-1)	$727.80
2000	Fusaichi Pegasus (2-1) & Aptitude (11-1)	$66.00
2001	Monarchos (10-1) & Invisible Ink (55-1)	$1229.00
2002	War Emblem (20-1) & Proud Citizen (23-1)	$1300.80
2003	Funny Cide (12-1) & Empire Maker (2-1) (my choice)	$97.00
2004	Smarty Jones (4-1) & Lion Heart (5-1)	$65.20
2005	Giacomo (50-1) & Closing Argument (71-1)	$9814.80
2006	Barbaro (6-1) (my choice) & Blue Grass Cat (30-1)	$587.00
2007	Street Sense (4-1) & Hard Spun (10-1)	$101.80
2008	Big Brown (2-1) & Eight Belles (13-1)	$141.60
2009	Mine That Bird (50-1) & Pioneer of the Nile (6-1)(mine)	$2074.80
2010	Super Saver (8-1) & Ice Box (11-1)	$152.40
2011	Animal Kingdom (21-1) & Nehro (8-1)(my choice)	$329.80
2012	I'll Have Another (15-1) & Bodemeister (4-1)	$306.60
2013	Orb (5-1) & Golden Soul (34-1)	$981.60
2014	California Chrome (2.5-1) & Commanding Curve (37-1)	$340
2015	American Pharoah (2.9-1) & Firing Line (9.5-1)	$72.60

This is why this Kentucky Derby exacta wager potentially is a great payout. If you choose five horses and box them together in a $2 exacta bet, it will cost you $40. For six horses it will cost $60. In 27 of the last 29 years, if you had made either of those bets, you would have made a healthy profit. In one of those years, you would have profited an amazing $9,812 for the $2 wager!

When I first started making the pilgrimage to Churchill Downs for Derby weekend, I loved watching the horses in the paddock area. Even though the crowds were large, my friends and I always made our way to the paddock. There used to be chairs and tables close by, and that was where we planted ourselves for the day. It was easy to see the televisions and we could walk out to the infield if we wanted. Most of us brought coolers with food so we didn't have to spend more money than necessary.

The paddock area is where we met the 'Jersey Boys' each year. A pleasant bunch of guys, they were fun, not too wild and crazy and exactly the types with whom we wanted to hang around. The group included my college roommate Frank Brabec and his wife Sheri, along with Frank's sister Teri and ex-husband Bob, fondly known around the track as 'Fireman Bob.' Bob was an ex-firefighter from Arlington Heights, who resided there in Louisville and had a job writing for one of the track publications. I was never one to pick Bob's horses, but I listened to him on occasion.

One time, Bob and I had a conversation regarding the ownership of Churchill Downs. I had expressed my interest in owning a piece of it, as I had seen attendance increase and more food and drinks being consumed. After asking him if he knew whether I could buy into Churchill Downs, he said the track in fact was privately-held and it was impossible for me to own a part of it. I then told Bob that I didn't think that was true, and it was a public company that was on the stock exchange. After doing some research and confirming to myself that I was right and he was wrong, I quickly discounted any of his further advice about anything.

In 1999, trainer Paul Magee invited Bob and Teri to the barns on Derby Day. They were told they could drive just one vehicle into the barn area, but they could have as many people in that vehicle as they could fit. So we all piled into his pickup with coolers, chairs and a truck-bed-full of people. It was a picture that looked like the Beverly Hillbillies in Louisville! We had at least eight people in the vehicle, some in the cab and others in the back of the truck. We passed through the gates and wound our way through the crowded barn area to a spot where an owner was having a pig roast party. What an experience that was! We spent the day mingling with owners, trainers and their guests, even visiting Magee's barns and enjoying a much different perspective than I had ever seen. But the one thing I do remember from that day is walking down the path and brushing shoulders with Tipper Gore, wife of the current U.S. Vice President Al Gore, who was a guest of Kentucky Governor Paul Patton. Flanked by four police officers, she was as friendly as could be. We crossed paths, smiled, exchanged pleasantries and just kept on walking.

You could place wagers in the barn area, but I quickly found out that there were the same long waiting lines as in the grandstands and infield. But the best part of the day was watching the Derby race from the back stretch as they came thundering down the track. They had set up special grandstands, allowing for a track perspective I'd never before enjoyed. I will never forget watching the race that day, as 'Charismatic' beat 'Menifee' by a neck. He went off at 31-1 odds and paid $64.60 to win. I wished I had that winner!

My sister, Shauna, and her husband Bert attended their first Derby in 2003. Up until then, I had always called my sister each year from a pay phone. Remember the pay phone? It's a piece of history some may not remember well, but one was installed under the grandstands, very close to the paddock. At that time, you could make a call anywhere in the United States for ten minutes and it cost a grand total of 25-cents. I would always call her from the paddock and discuss the horses as she watched from the comfort of her living room in Santa Clarita, California. It was nice that I could facilitate my sister being a part of the Derby experience it from afar. Shauna used to watch the entire day of racing on NBC as they televised the action. I also would mention during our phone conversations about attending the Derby in-person, but she never did --until 2003. That year Churchill Downs had offered some additional bleacher-style seating inside the infield, facing the regular grandstands. It offered the flavor of the infield with the comfort of seats. I loved that perspective, as we were able to spend time walking around the infield, seeing the sights, and then make our way quickly back to our seats to see the race. The views from these infield seating were outstanding and simply breathtaking. You saw the crowds, the winners circle and the spires. In addition, the fans in the stands were much more civil than the party people in the infield. It was fantastic because it was so easy to move around. Unfortunately, these seats were in place for only a few years.

That year, 2003, I had picked 'Empire Maker' to win the Derby. His odds were 2-1, but I still thought he was the best horse in the race even though, as I previously stated, I generally avoid betting on favorites in the Derby. Interestingly, 'Empire Maker' was sired by 1990 Derby winner 'Unbridled,' and was the grandsire of 2016 Triple Crown winner 'American Pharoah.' My sister liked 'Funny Cide,' a 12-1 longshot. She decided to box an exacta with 'Empire Maker' for $5. I was curious why she bet that horse, but I have since learned to listen to her and respect her perspective. I still would not necessarily pick her horses to win, but I absolutely will look at them and try to better understand her thought process. As it happened, beginners luck hit and she won the exacta for $242.50. From now on, I always will listen to my sister and try to include her horses with mine. I won't want to miss out on another big exacta payoff.

I have always enjoyed Derby Weekend in Louisville. And things have really changed a lot since 1974. From the Red Barn to the Red Roof Inn, from camping and motor homes to hotels and warm showers, it only has gotten better. But there are two things that will never change: horse race fans dressed to the nines and those young and crazy kids in the infield. The Derby always is a great place to 'people watch.'

Each year is different. When I first started going to the Kentucky Derby, I could walk right up to the rail of the racetrack. I can still remember the exhilarating feeling with the ground shaking as the horses thundered by me in the final turn before they headed down that last quarter of a mile. But as the years went on, Churchill Downs made changes to make it safer for the riders and their horses as they race around the track. They put up a fence just on the outside of the railing between the infield and the track. It probably was for the best. For those of us who were there and experienced it the old way, it was fantastic.

I strongly encourage everyone to attend the Kentucky Derby at least once in your lifetime. I am sure that once you do so, you will want to return to Louisville each year. Make your experience a memorable one. Make it a multiple-day event. Check out the Pegasus parade on Thursday, enjoy the steamboat race on the river Wednesday night before the Derby, visit the Louisville Baseball Bat factory or take a bourbon tour. Enjoy a round of golf or take in the local wineries. But whatever you do, be sure to get down to Louisville, Kentucky, for the Derby, held the first Saturday in May each year. You won't regret it.

CHAPTER 12

THE PAYOFF

It's my hope that in reading this book, you take away all the basic information you need in order to make 'Smarter Bets – The Exacta Way.' The majority of this book was written with the beginner or intermediate handicapper in mind.

It's my personal preference to bet exactas. If you narrow it down to the top three horses, you will maximize your bets and come home with the most money.

Everybody loves to pick a winner. You can brag about it, you sound like you know what you're doing and you can impress your friends. But you may find that the most rewarding aspect of making smarter bets is the financial return on your investment.

If you make an effort to spend the time to prepare for the races, like I do, you'll find that it will give you the best chance to win.

I've really enjoyed the entire process, as I think you will, too. Plan your outing to the racetrack, spend the time and effort handicapping the horses, be sure to go there with good friends, bet only the races that you feel you'll have the best chance of winning, and you'll end up coming home with a smile on your face.

As I've explained, there are a number of different types of wagers you can make. Some are easier than others and some are riskier. But with the handicapping information included in this book, I think you have an advantage!

Another important thing to remember is that you can't win every race. By using my system and rationales I've included in this book, I believe you will be able to identify the best races on which to bet. Keep in mind that you only have so much money to bet with, and it's important to manage your money wisely. By following this process, it should maximize your investment. Looking over my 'dirty dozen' considerations will guide you in that respect.

There are additional aspects and special angles that many experienced handicappers use. For example, they may notice that some trainers do very well with first-time starters while other trainers have better results with second-time starters.

As you become more experienced, you'll accumulate knowledge about patterns, trainer habits and general information that will help you formulate your own system and identify your top choices.

The exotic wagers, including exactas, are more complicated, but with a better payoff. For some handicappers, this is more alluring. Even if exacta wagering is not for you, it's my hope that you gain enough knowledge from this book to help you in your next visit to the track.

This is the second edition printing of my first book. I'd like to make you aware of the second book in the series, 'Inside the Sport of Kings,' which includes perspectives, insights, interviews and some of my favorite stories. With many interesting facts and anecdotes, it will provide you some fascinating background as you become more engaged with the sport.

Some of the chapters talk about how pace makes the race, the physical appearance of a horse, along with fun insights on betting. I've taken the time to interview or provide perspectives on horse ownership groups like Midwest Thoroughbreds, Drawing Away Stables and successful female horse owner Maggie Moss. Being a predominantly male sport, I've addressed women in horse racing, including the first generation of female jockeys and agents.

Also included are personal interviews with well-known track announcer John G. Dooley and well-respected trainer Dale Bennett.

I'm in the process of writing my third book, which is targeted for later in 2016. Be sure to look for it on Amazon!

All of my books may be found on Amazon. You also can visit my websites www.thederbyfan.com and www.keiththederbyman.com.

Thanks for reading – see you at the track!

Smarter Bets – The Exacta Way

Friends gather with track announcer Luke Kruytbosch (deceased) at Paul McGee's barn – Kentucky Derby 2000.

My sister, Shauna, and her husband Bert at their first Kentucky Derby along with other friends – 2003.

The University of Louisville Marching Band plays "My Old Kentucky Home" before the 129th running of the Kentucky Derby.

A recent photo of my horse, "Little Michael" in the winner's circle at Arlington International Racecourse, 2013.

Printed in Great Britain
by Amazon